JOYCE'S OCKENDEN

The Story of a Vision
that became a
Venture for Refugees

PAMELA WATKIN

Broadmead Paperback

Pamela Watkin attended Bedford College, London University. Her English teaching career included two years at Woking County School, where Joyce Pearce had once been a head girl, and twelve years at Woking Sixth Form College. She is married with a daughter and two sons.

First Published in 1993 by Broadmead Press
IBSN 0 9520988 0 6

© Pamela Watkin 1993

Published for The Ockenden Venture,
Constitution Hill, Woking, Surrey GU22 7UU
by Broadmead Press, 124 High Street,
Old Woking, Surrey GU22 9JN

All rights reserved

Printed and bound in Great Britain by
Unwin Brothers Ltd, The Gresham Press,
Old Woking

Typesetting by Timothy and Lalage Watkin

To the Ockenden family
worldwide

Contents

1	An End and a Beginning	1
2	Welcome to "Ockenden"!	3
3	Formative Years	7
4	The First Venture	11
5	The German Camps	16
6	Vision Extended	25
7	The First Great Blossoming	34
8	Donington Days	45
9	The Plight of Tibet	49
10	Journey to the Tibetans	54
11	Tibetan Venture	66
12	Out of South Africa	74
13	A School in the Desert	80
14	The Saddest Chapter	91
15	An Evil the World Allowed	94
16	Project Vietnam	103
17	Ockenden's Second Great Blossoming	121
18	Life in The Sudan	132

19 An Ashram in East Bengal	147
20 Thai Payap	153
21 The Afghans in Pakistan	160
22 Solidarity with Poland	167
23 A Strategy of Hope for a World in Crisis	178

Foreword

Joyce Pearce, the inspiration of Ockenden, died in 1985. She left behind a great number of friends in many different walks of life. She also left a wonderful work accomplished for refugees and other disadvantaged people, as well as some unfinished business which those of us left behind hoped we might complete. She left, too, a mountainous archive of letters, articles, speeches, newspaper cuttings, memorabilia, photographs, accounts of her journeys, stories of her meetings with the famous and the lowly.

When our grief began to be assuaged by the passage of time, we, her friends, began our labour of love through the enchanted forest of paper. Her former Secretaries, Assistants and friends, Oonagh Guyonnet, Rita Comerford, Jane Cambridge, Janka Stuttard, worked valiantly at filing, sorting, deciphering, and I made an attempt to put some of it together, with the help of Denise Moll, Joyce's last Secretary. We might have been toiling on until the year 2000 had not Pamela Watkin offered her services as a writer. She had long known of The Ockenden Venture; she had had two brief stays at Ockenden houses as a volunteer years before; she had enjoyed writing her first book, *A Kingston Lacy Childhood*; she would attempt her second book if we would help her and give her access to files. We gave her all the help we could — the fruit of our own labours and access to other material — but she would have months of delving, interviewing and sorting wheat from chaff.

After eighteen months' concentrated endeavour, she gave me the manuscript to read, to alter and shorten if necessary, to comment on. All I've done, apart from some minor changes, is to enjoy it. What I have found most incredible is her ability to present a picture of the Joyce we all knew so well, but whom she had never met; to enter into the Spirit of Ockenden; to enter into the mystery of Joyce.

Margaret Dixon, Woking 1993.

1 An End and a Beginning

"You are wonderful!" said Joyce Pearce, "Wonderful!", as a telephone call from His Holiness the Dalai Lama, the exiled temporal and spiritual leader of Tibet, lifted her thoughts high above the pain of her last illness.

Ever since their first meeting in India twenty years before, when Joyce had gone there to help refugee Tibetan children, she and the Dalai Lama had been friends. Not only had they responded to each other's profound compassion. They had also delighted in each other's sense of fun.

Despite the differences between her Christian and his Buddhist beliefs, the outlooks of the English school teacher and the learned Tibetan monk were remarkably similar. His Holiness wanted every individual selflessly to promote the happiness of others, so enabling the whole human family to reach contentment. This teaching harmonised perfectly with Christ's message of brotherly love which, from the start, inspired Joyce's sharing vision.

The call from His Holiness, in May 1985, almost the last telephone call Joyce ever received, made her ready to accept escape to a higher plane, trusting in God to take care of her Ockenden Venture. Soon after she died, her faithful old black labrador, Minnie, having, it seemed, not the slightest intention of parting from her, died too.

Ockenden's staff and committee, together with rich, poor, famous and unknown friends of many nationalities, poured into Westminster Abbey for Joyce's memorial service, many wondering how, without her, their little vessel of refugees would keep afloat. Reassuringly, they remembered what Joyce herself always said. Notwithstanding the admiration she received for her work and the OBE she was awarded, it had been a loving power, far stronger than her own drive and energy, that had launched The Ockenden Venture.

When Joyce set off from Woking to London, early one August morning in 1951, to meet seventeen "displaced" teenagers at Liverpool Street Station, she had simply no idea what lay ahead.

2 Welcome to "Ockenden"!

Joyce Pearce and Rotarians from Woking easily picked out "their" East Europeans from other passengers descending from the Harwich steam train. In foreign clothes, wrinkled and creased after a long journey across Germany, those excited-looking youngsters, escorted by a slim, tired-looking English girl, could only be refugees.

The young people's faces lit up as a small, round lady with dark hair and glasses hurried towards them, closely followed by the Rotarians and some newspaper reporters. She must be "Miss Purse," they thought, the English school teacher who had spirited them out of their sordid refugee camps for a fortnight's holiday.

Seeing the youngsters suddenly the focus of attention, passing day-trippers, hundreds of whom were pouring into London for the Festival of Britain, glanced curiously at them, probably not guessing that they were refugees. It was six whole years since the end of World War Two. Having thrown off post-war gloom, so far from wondering what might have happened to displaced Nazi victims, the British were in Festival mood, looking forward to the rides and slides of Battersea Funfair and to gazing at the vertical steel "Skylon" hanging in the air over the South Bank. They could have been forgiven for assuming that, by now, the United Nations must have sorted out the problem of European refugees.

The teenagers gazed around the smoky station, hardly able to believe they were in England and off to "Miss Purse's" home in Surrey. They were in far too euphoric a state of mind to remember any English words, or even to respond to Joyce's fluent German.

Then a Rotarian noticed that a sturdy Lithuanian boy in a bowler hat was carrying a violin. "Can you play us something?" he mimed, moving one arm up and down across the other. Fourteen-year-old Herkules grinned. With great panache, he brought his part of the station to a halt, as people stopped to listen to his unexpected, virtuoso performance of *Perpetuum Mobile*.

The refugees laughed and clapped. What fun to have one of their number showing off his talent in front of a crowd of people, including sheltered–looking English girls, immaculately dressed in crisp cotton frocks and affluent–seeming English boys in tweed jackets and smartly pressed grey flannels!

Saying goodbye to their at that time unknown young escort, Sue Ryder, and detaching themselves from the reporters, the seventeen Estonians, Latvians, Lithuanians and Poles followed Joyce and the Rotarians out of Liverpool Street Station and across London to Waterloo and the Woking train. As they arrived at Woking, a cheer went up from a line of flag–waving, green–uniformed school girls waiting on the platform. Small hands darted out to grab the refugees' suitcases. Then, with much high–pitched chatter, they were escorted down White Rose Lane to "Ockenden," Joyce's home.

Rambling, red–brick and Victorian, "Ockenden" was surrounded by four acres of wild garden, with trees calling out to be climbed, lawns waiting to have balls kicked around on them and leafy, secluded paths to be explored.

The interior of the house was equally enticing. Margaret Dixon, Joyce's friend, and three teacher volunteers from England, France and Norway, who had spent hours polishing floors and furniture, had filled every available vase and bowl with carnations.

One or two teenagers brushed away a tear as they walked around under the high, moulded ceilings. Few could remember ever being inside a house before. Mirdza, the eldest, thought of the large, beautiful home in Latvia which her father had owned before the war, when he had been an accountant in a silk factory. First the Russians, then the Germans had invaded. Then her whole family had been taken for forced labour. Austra, Mirdza's flaxen–haired, fourteen–year–old sister, walking with her into "Ockenden," had been born in a camp.

Hercules surprises everyone at Liverpool Street Station in 1951

"Ockenden," White Rose Lane, Woking

In "Ockenden's" easy atmosphere, the young refugees from eight different, isolated camps in Germany became united and talkative. The girls luxuriated in deep baths, washing their hair under undreamed of, endless gushes of hot water. Freed from the restrictions of the camps, the boys revelled in roaming the garden and the public park next door.

First thing every morning, Woking well-wishers deposited salad, vegetables, eggs and meat on the doorstep so that Margaret Dixon, who organised the meals, never needed money from the holiday fund for food. Provisions continued to be stacked in front of the door, even when news came that Sue Ryder could not be spared from relief work in Germany to collect the teenagers and the planned fortnight's holiday lengthened into a month.

With Margaret, who spoke just enough German not to be taken advantage of, Ruth Hicks, Joyce's other close friend, who had a calming effect on the most boisterous behaviour, and the three young teachers, Joyce kept firm control of the ebullient household. Yet she continually dissolved it into shrieks of laughter with her multifarious, multi-lingual mishaps.

On one of several group expeditions to the Festival of Britain, to Joyce's consternation, the party's young violinist disappeared, to be found an hour later sprawling on the steps of the Pavilion of Discovery licking an ice cream. The teenagers screeched with delight at Joyce's description of the disbelief on the face of a policeman as she told him she was searching for someone she knew only as "Herkules."

Every evening, Joyce, teenagers and teacher helpers gathered round Margaret at the piano and Herkules with his violin to sing all the songs they knew in their various languages. The last, most pensively sung number in the joyful, spirited repertoire was always,

Que sera sera,
Whatever will be will be,

summing up the young people's stoical attitude.

None of the refugees could envisage permanent escape from their camps. Unlike French, Dutch and Belgian Nazi victims, who had been repatriated after being released from slave labour and concentration camps at the end of the war, East Europeans could not go home. Their countries had now passed into communist control. Though the United Nations Relief and Rehabilitation Administration (UNRRA) had resettled many in Western countries with labour shortages, thousands remained marooned in Austria and Germany. In the case of Joyce's young guests, this was because someone in each of their families had failed the medical test for emigration. Families who refused to abandon their sick members had to stay where they were, leading a squalid existence in the unhealthy camps.

When she had time to think about it, Joyce was amazed that seventeen displaced teenagers of four different nationalities were being refreshed and invigorated at "Ockenden."

Remembering the burst of sympathy she and some English sixth formers had felt on first hearing about young East European refugees, she believed it had been the work of the Holy Spirit, projecting them into an extraordinary energy field of human generosity which she later called the "networking." "All right then," she would say afterwards, to non-Christian friends who could not relate to her talk about the Holy Spirit, "Let's just say it was the Spirit of Love."

3   Formative Years

Joyce was born on November 23rd 1915 into a Woking family. Though Henry Quartermaine, her grandfather, engineer and entrepreneur, owned "half the town," her parents passed on to her a totally non-acquisitive attitude to money. It was a matter of pride to her mother, that, so far from having been spoiled by her privileged childhood, she could manage her household perfectly well on a limited income, in the small flat above her husband's radio shop in the town centre.

Running the shop in Chertsey Road gave Vic Pearce, Joyce's father, the opportunity to meet people, leaving him plenty of energy to play golf and tennis and be a famous member of Woking's football team, and plenty of time to enjoy a drink and smoke with friends. Later he became leader of the Home Guard and a member of the Chamber of Commerce.

While Joyce inherited Vic Pearce's easy-going, fun-loving nature, the deep seriousness, which was also part of her character, came from her mother. Mary Pearce had been brought up in a tradition of public service, for "Grandy" Quartermaine, her father, was a Justice of the Peace and three times Chairman of Woking Council. During World War One, she began a long Red Cross career as a VAD nurse in the Middlesex Hospital, leaving Joyce in the care of a maid.

Without brothers or sisters and with just Prince, her dog, to play with, Joyce developed a habit of contemplation, losing herself in books, living, as she said, "in a dream." Naturally happy, she could not help worrying about the "war-wounded" soldiers and civilians her mother was looking after.

Mary Pearce sowed the seeds of Joyce's Christian faith, telling her of spiritual healings she had witnessed in her nursing work. Belief in the healing power of prayer was reinforced by Ruth Hicks, Mary's gentle cousin, who came to live in Woking when Joyce was seven.

At first Joyce studied with a governess shared with another family. At the age of eleven she went to the local girls' grammar school, where Ruth Hicks was mathematics teacher and deputy head. Woking County School for girls, which many years later was rehoused in a dignified red brick building, consisted at that time only of a few Nissen huts separated by mud. Yet it already had a strong academic tradition. Joyce's intelligent mind was stimulated by excellent teaching and she became a keen hockey player and a pianist. Her kindly, responsible, gregarious nature endearing her to girls and staff alike, in 1933 she became Head Girl. Yet in private she still quietly worried about human suffering — especially suffering that was man-made, wondering why people should want to inflict pain upon one another.

In the hope of finding out how much moral progress mankind had made and how much more progress was possible, Joyce applied to read for an Oxford history degree at Lady Margaret Hall.

Oxford provided inspiring role models, including the Vice Principal of Lady Margaret Hall, Miss Jamison, whose interests, not confined to her special subject, the Normans in Italy, ranged over art, poetry, philosophy, nature and politics. Joyce did not consider it intrusively moralistic when, like her mother, Miss Jamison urged her, "Make sure the world is a little better for your having been in it."

Another of Joyce's heroines, interesting in the light of her future world-wanderings, was the intrepid Miss Grier, Principal of Lady Margaret Hall, who, at the age of sixty, crossed Mongolia on the back of a mule. Even more significant was Joyce's meeting with Dr Schweitzer, scientist, explorer, musician and missionary, who spoke of the growing phenomenon of refugees.

Dr Schweitzer warned that political conflicts, repressive attitudes and a progressively unfair distribution of resources between North and South, would cause a movement of peoples in the modern world greater than any in recorded time. He himself, he said, half jokingly, kept by him the address of an Ethiopian traveller he had met, in case he should need it, for "Who knows who may become a refugee in this century, from what or when?"

Throughout her time at Oxford, Joyce wrestled with the realities of good and evil. Years later, C.S. Lewis wrote to congratulate her on a letter she had sent him as a student. He said she seemed to have reached the conclusions of the best theologians on her own.

"Oh, dear!" she thought, "If only I could remember what I wrote!" for she had not kept a copy of her letter. She supposed it must have been along the lines of C. S. Lewis' comments, with which she agreed, that the great experiment of the cosmos was the gift to Man of creative action combined with free will. Man, free to aspire to the absolute perfection in which the whole hierarchy of angels and archangels are held, through pride and self-interest often chooses to associate himself with powers of darkness.

"It is inconceivable that Nature, as we see it, is either what God intended or merely evil," wrote C.S.Lewis. "It looks like a good thing spoiled. The doctrine of the Fall (both of man and of some 'gods' or 'angels') is the only satisfactory explanation. Though freedom is real, it is not infinite. Every choice reduces a little one's freedom to choose next time. There finally comes a time when the creature is fully built, irrevocably attached either to God or to itself."

To Joyce, deeply conscious from an early age of the "war-wounded," the most evil choice of all was of mass murder, legitimised by the name of war. She was not alone. The Oxford students who in 1933 had voted, "This House will on no account fight for King and Country," were still undergraduates, now organising pacifist meetings and demonstrations in which Joyce herself took part.

Yet, could what two refugee Jewish academics said in the Senior Common Room about evil deeds committed just across the Channel in Germany be true? If so, what should Britain do about it?

Joyce vowed not to engage in any warlike activity herself. After obtaining her degree, she took an Oxford education diploma, then temporary teaching posts at Reigate, Chichester and Launceston in Cornwall, discovering that she liked and got on extremely well with children.

While Joyce was in Chichester, Britain declared war on Germany. An evil energy was let loose in the Western world. Joyce took comfort from surges of bravery and compassion that sometimes overcame negative forces of fear and bitterness. Nationalistic hatred could turn to sympathy in a moment, when people actually saw an enemy and realised that he was human. Proof of this came when one of her pupils found a German airman, having escaped from his crashed Messerschmitt, staggering around the school field. The girl took him home to her parents who looked after him solicitously, making sure he had fully recovered before bringing him back for Joyce to take to the police.

So many permanent teaching posts were available while men were on active service, that Joyce became a very young senior history mistress in Mitcham Girls' Grammar School. As she invigilated examinations during air-raids, in shelters so cramped that it was almost impossible for the candidates not to cheat, she thought bitterly that her generation of history undergraduates had been the last of the innocents. Never again would the young expect modern technology to eliminate poverty and oppression. Advanced technology was being directed against people. So far from mankind's becoming more enlightened, news was seeping out that a barbarism as great as any in the Middle Ages had been perpetrated in the concentration camps of Belsen, Dachau, Sachsenhausen, Mautheusen, Ravensbruck, Auschwitz and Buchenwald, confirming the worst stories of the Jewish refugees.

When Hiroshima and Nagasaki extinguished huge swathes of humanity, the last comforting certainties about human behaviour were swept away. Mankind had a hitherto unimaginable will and capacity for destruction. Could one still believe in God or in any ultimate good?

4 The First Venture

To help them come to terms with the implications of the horrors through which they were living, Joyce encouraged her sixth form pupils to talk about them. It quickly became apparent that forty-minute periods were too short. Long after the bell had sounded for the end of the lesson, much more always remained to be said. Joyce decided to host open-ended discussion sessions at weekends in her own home.

Margaret Dixon, geography teacher and Mitcham Grammar School's redoubtable deputy head, who had been sharing Joyce's small Streatham flat ever since her own flat had been bombed, was in favour of Joyce's idea. Margaret's ideas about education had changed too. With the whole world in turmoil and human nature being revealed in a terrible new light, how could one continue force-feeding girls with facts to make them win university scholarships?

Margaret approved of Joyce's innovatory practice of encouraging sixth formers to lift their eyes from the hallowed examination syllabus to observe what was going on in the outside world — in the Law Courts or the Council offices. She defended her when other teachers criticised the time spent "going out with those girls!". Equally supportive at home, Margaret looked after the cooking, which she enjoyed, but about which Joyce, her mind usually upon higher things, was sometimes a little vague. Margaret was determined that Joyce, whose respect for all life made her a vegetarian, should nevertheless have nourishing meals.

Mentally agile, witty and uncompromisingly direct, Margaret took a lively interest in the girls' discussions of such topics as justice and peace, about which she too cared passionately. She had learned concern for the poor and indignation about war at her mother's knee. On the other hand, with her flair for literature, music and drama, she regarded discussion itself as a form of art.

The discussions came to seem increasingly important as more and more seventeen- and eighteen-year-old girls began regularly squeezing into the small flat. In the spring of 1947, as Joyce was racking her brains about how to cope with such large numbers, she received a call from her mother. "Why don't you use 'Ockenden' for your discussions?"

Mrs Pearce had taken out a mortgage on "Ockenden" — whose name came from the Anglo-Saxon words for Oak-in-the-valley — on the strength of some of "Grandy" Quartermaines's securities which she held in trust. She had intended to turn it into a nursing home combining natural and spiritual healing but, to her disappointment, her bishop disapproved. She would back-track on the idea for a while. Meantime, how convenient if Joyce could take over the house!

In vain Joyce protested that a teacher's monthly wage of £28 would not pay rates or a mortgage. "Do just come and look at it, Joyce dear!" her mother urged.

Joyce instantly saw "Ockenden's" possibilities. The dark red dining room and sombre brown woodwork could be transformed by bright paint. Light flooded in through tall, wide windows overlooking a garden where daffodils danced under the trees. In summer the rooms would be cool and airy; in winter, cosy, with log fires crackling in the wide stone hearths. An upstairs billiards room would make a dormitory. Equally conveniently, the house was only five minutes from the main line station and beside Woking park with tennis courts and an open air pool.

With Ruth Hicks and Margaret Dixon promising to share responsibility, Joyce decided to open "Ockenden" as a residential sixth form centre. Sixth formers would be able to listen to speakers well-informed about topics not touched on in school. They would be given a basis of facts, then encouraged to think for themselves, no attempt being made to indoctrinate them. Each student would pay ten shillings per weekend to cover running expenses, for neither Margaret nor Joyce had any resources apart from their teaching salaries. Ruth had no money at all, having resigned from teaching to nurse a sick friend, investing her savings in "Beechlands," a large Woking house in Brooklyn Road.

"Beechlands" had already provided Ruth with experience of running a residential community. In wartime it had sheltered not only Joyce's parents (while Mrs Pearce was organising mobile medical units as a Commandant for the Red Cross and Vic Pearce working with the Home Guard), but also Ruth's own mother, two ancient uncles, a distant, profoundly deaf, aged relative called Maud, three "billeted" Canadian officers, a Russian emigreé with a parrot, an old-fashioned cook-housekeeper and Winifred, the cook's helper, with her baby.

Joyce and Margaret often escaped from war-oppressed Streatham to "Beechlands" at weekends, attending Mrs Pearce's Friday evening healing services in an "upper room." Victims of Parkinson's disease, disseminated sclerosis, stress or old age came to be strengthened and comforted, sitting on soft blue chairs in front of a shining brass cross. The services always began with the hymn, "Dear Lord and Father of Mankind" and ended with "O Love that wilt not let me go," Margaret bellowing the words into Maud's ear so that she could take part.

With "Ockenden" still empty, apart from some huge items of furniture from her great uncle's former home in Maidenhead, Joyce, wanting allies on her school staff, invited younger teachers from Mitcham to camp out in the house for a weekend. Romping in the echoing rooms and strolling among the bluebells in the wild garden, they felt as if they were in the country. In the evening, wrapping themselves in red blankets which Mrs Pearce had donated, they sat on the dusty floor discussing ideas for sixth form weekends.

By the beginning of the new school year, the old house had been turned into a comfortable conference centre. Mitcham teachers and sixth formers had washed, scrubbed, painted and polished it and rubbed up the brass on the solid oak doors. Joyce, Margaret and Ruth had installed new carpets and begged and bought second-hand furniture, comfortable armchairs, ex–Army camp beds, grey blankets and mattresses. While wanting to prepare sixth formers for the austerity of a university hall of residence, Joyce also aimed to create a homely setting conducive to lofty thought.

****

"But why should we want to go to Woking?" asked Mitcham's new sixth formers. One or two reluctantly agreed to take part in the first conference on what was then known as "The Colour Bar," to which two Jamaican students from London University were going to contribute. More sixth formers were drawn from Woking, Wallington and East Ham. To their surprise, even the Mitcham students found it exhilarating to identify a problem, then discuss its causes, ramifications and solutions. Girls who were too shy to speak in scheduled discussions turned into debaters while washing up or taking their turn to peel potatoes.

After this first success, Joyce summoned school heads and the Chief Surrey Education Officer to a briefing meeting about the extra dimension which "Ockenden" weekends would add to the education system. Mrs Pearce invited Dr Vidler, Canon of St George's Chapel, Windsor, whom she had met on a theological course he was directing at William Temple College, the first theological college for women. A "sceptic in faith's clothing," Dr Vidler was a well-known advocate of honest debate with faith and doubt standing side by side.

Joyce was as successful as her mother in making prominent people see the value of what she wanted to do. Running his finger down the long list of acceptances for the meeting, Dr Vidler laughed, "I shall feel a great fraud among so many swells." He became chairman of a group of sponsors who produced a leaflet and formally established The Ockenden Centre.

"Ockenden" weekends became famous, with sixty schools participating from as far afield as Liverpool, Lincolnshire and Sheffield. Joyce was toying with the idea of giving up teaching and organising the courses full time, when her father's death in May 1948, three days after an operation for cancer, precipitated her decision.

To cope with her grief, she would change direction, packing her life with meaning and activity. Handing in her notice at school and leaving Margaret in sole occupation of the Streatham flat, she moved into "Ockenden."

5 The German Camps

Joyce devoted all her time to the discussion weekends which became even more inspiring than before, with eminent religious leaders, musicians, writers, philosophers, artists, poets and university lecturers and leading politicians and statesmen taking part. Though almost all secondary schools were still segregated, the Ockenden Sixth Form Centre became co–educational.

Costs increased, in spite of the fact that Joyce did the shopping and most of the cleaning and Margaret cooked the meals. Just in time to prevent their running into debt, for they refused to raise students' fees, Joyce and Ruth Hicks were offered the good will of Greenfield, a private girls' school, part of "Grandy" Quartermaine's estate, on the other side of Woking park. Ruth, whose sick friend had died, became headmistress, with Joyce, a "sleeping" partner, doing some part–time teaching.

Shortly after this, in June 1951, during an Ockenden film appreciation weekend, a film was shown called *An Answer for Anne*, about a young girl's struggle to persuade her American village to accept an immigrant family. It included footage of displaced persons' camps in West Germany. For the first time, the English sixth formers were aware of thousands of teenagers like themselves living in squalid conditions just across the Channel, with no hope of education or employment.

Displaced people were relegated to former German army barracks, situated far away from industrial centres where refugees might have found work. Consequently they had no salaries and no money to pay for their children's education. National secondary schools, which refugees set up in some camps, closed as their teachers emigrated.

Angry and upset at the injustice, the sixth formers wondered what they could do to help. "Could we give some of them a holiday?" they wondered. They discussed the idea with intensity but, by Sunday evening, when it was time to go home, nothing had been resolved. The idea seemed to have trailed away in words.

Yet it was still there, hovering in the air. Joyce could not forget it.

A day or so later, a strange coincidence occurred. Joyce happened to mention the idea of the holiday to Mrs Banham, the local vicar's wife, who came to ask if she could host a guide camp at "Ockenden." Mrs Banham happened to be English International Commissioner of the Guides International Service. GIS happened to be working in the British zone of Germany, trying with the Red Cross to clear up social problems created by the war.

Mrs Banham contacted Dame Rosa Ward, GIS's formidable founder, who telephoned Gwen Hesketh, the Australian in charge of GIS welfare work in Hamburg, but there the idea seemed to stop. Gwen's response was, "Oh, no! It would be like taking a bird out of its cage, then putting it back again."

Well, at least she would visit the camps, Joyce thought sadly. Then she received a startling call. Could she take between sixteen and twenty teenagers in August? If so, would she say yes at once? Could she guarantee their fares and maintenance? She asked for just two hours to think it over.

As yet Woking had no original plan for celebrating the Festival of Britain. Joyce rang Mrs Banham. Did Mrs Banham think Woking...? Yes, she did. Joyce rang GIS. Yes, of course she could raise the money! That night, having accepted financial responsibility for a holiday for up to twenty teenagers, neither she nor Mrs Banham could sleep.

Fortunately, Woking Council was intrigued by the thought of such an unusual way of celebrating the Festival. Mrs Walker, the organiser of Woking's music club, persuaded her husband to become the treasurer of a holiday fund, and the Walkers and Joyce staged a public meeting, sending individual invitations to local government officials, clergy, managers of local organisations and fifty influential people from the town. Everyone came. Everyone wanted to help.

An appeal in the *Woking News and Mail* produced donations from factories, families, the Guides, schools and the Round Table — enough for the children's fares and, if used economically, for their maintenance too. Miss Hesketh phoned from Germany to say the youngsters who had been selected for the holiday were "too thrilled to speak."

****

Once the displaced children had settled in at "Ockenden," they found it comforting to exchange experiences. They had so much in common, especially their longing for education.

Mirdza knew it was far too late to achieve her ambition of becoming a doctor. In 1944, when the Russians, who had previously been expelled from Latvia by the Germans, had returned, her family had been taken to a labour camp in Germany. A Russian dive-bomb attack on their ship had injured her leg, yet she had been made to work thirteen hours a day. When she finally collapsed, her leg was found to be tubercular. It took three years to heal. Never having had the chance to go to school, she was entirely self-educated.

Sixteen-year-old Bireta also fruitlessly longed to be a doctor. Her Lithuanian camp school was not of a high enough standard for her to reach the level of a German medical course. Another Lithuanian, Luidas, demonstrated a keen interest in English literature, asking Joyce to show him places connected with Sir Walter Scott, Byron, Oscar Wilde and Shakespeare.

Herkules, the most confident of all the young people even though his mother had died just a few days before he came to England, could not accept the professional training on offer for him in America, because his father, the very person who had taught him the violin, had TB.

Perhaps the keenest of all of them to go to school was Janina, a tall, fifteen-year-old who had been taken away from home when she was seven. She had made good progress in her Polish camp school until it had closed, leaving her with just two books which she had brought to "Ockenden" — a Polish-Latin grammar and *Alice in Wonderland* in English.

The refugees' visit to Woking made British people in general more conscious of displaced people. The teenagers were written about in the local and national press and Mirdza and Herkules were selected for the popular radio programme *In Town Tonight*. Everyone crowded round the big brown radio at "Ockenden" to listen to John Ellison interviewing them and to Herkules playing *Perpetuum Mobile*.

The group was almost smothered by the whole-hearted outpouring of hospitality of Woking people. A cinema gave them all weekly free seats and families invited them into their homes, finding it moving to watch even the older ones enjoying playing with children's toys which had previously been outside their experience.

Local sixth formers arrived every evening to join in games, conversation and singing, inviting the refugees to youth clubs, picnics, camp fires and fancy dress parties. The Round Table Association gave the whole group dinner at Heathrow Airport and showed them over an airliner, and individuals took two or three at a time to the National Gallery, the British Museum, Book Exhibitions, the Latvian Song Festival in the Albert Hall, the Ice Ballet at Harringay, the Searchlight Tattoo on Horse Guards Parade and to London Zoo. On their many group expeditions to London, the refugees rode up and down as many escalators as possible, never growing used to the size of London's population, which, from the top of Westminster Cathedral, seemed four times as great as that of all Latvia.

Mirdza and Ida were old enough to have been to the theatre before the war: the others had seen only amateur entertainments in camp huts. It was a magical experience for them to attend the International Ballet Company's performance of *The Sleeping Princess* in the Festival

Hall and to stand outside on the balcony in the interval, watching the lights of the Festival and the South Bank.

Yet neither the refugees nor their friends could forget that the respite from camp life was only temporary. As Canon Venables of Windsor was showing the young people round the Garter Chapel, he was asked by one the significance of two ladies holding anchors beside a cracked globe on Lord Linlithgow's shield. He was in tears as he explained that the figures signified Hope — "If all the world should crack, still Hope remains."

For the refugees' last night in Woking, fifty friends were invited to a party in return for their hospitality. In a celebration tinged with sadness, they consumed mountains of sandwiches, cakes and trifle, played games, danced and sang in the garden. Mirdza and Austra added to the brave carnival atmosphere by wearing their colourful national costumes.

When the last guest had gone, the refugees announced, "Anyone who goes to sleep tonight will have his face blacked with soot!" Next morning, only one boy appeared with a black nose. The others had played cards and indulged in last hot baths until four o'clock in the morning, when Joyce had crept downstairs and turned off the electricity.

Thirty years later, Janina and Herkules were among people celebrating Joyce's story on the television programme *This Is Your Life*. Though Joyce had co-operated in a similar programme about Sue Ryder, she was shocked and embarrassed to be confronted herself at the entrance to the National Theatre by Eamonn Andrews, complete with large red folder and microphone, and driven to a television studio. She had just had an abscess lanced and it was painful to smile. Worse still, though she was in evening dress, having expected to appear on stage with Peter Ustinov to talk about refugees, she had no time to take off her winter boots.

All the same, how wonderful to be reunited with some of her refugees! Herkules' father had recovered, allowing his whole family to emigrate. Now Herkules was a member of an American orchestra. On behalf of all the refugees, Herkules said that their first holiday in England had opened a window onto the world.

When the window swung shut again, Woking's schools and youth clubs could only promise to send parcels to the refugees to show they were not forgotten and to enable them to spread some Christmas cheer around their camps.

For Margaret and Joyce, the "holiday" lasted longer. It had been a waste of time for them to plan a few recuperative days in Italy before the new school term. Instead, they were irresistibly projected into a greater involvement with refugees. Having received a telephone message that Sue Ryder was still too busy to come to Woking and that her replacement as escort had broken her leg, they realised they themselves would have to accompany the children back to Germany. Waved away by tearful, tired friends, the party set off next evening. As well as their cases, the boys carried rucksacks full of hard boiled eggs, drinks and sandwiches, which Margaret had packed up for everyone.

At first all went well. The refugees were delighted to find that Joyce had booked first-class cabins. Only on arrival in the Hook of Holland did things begin to go wrong. Margaret opened the rucksacks to find that they were empty. The boys had already eaten all the food! The rest of the journey was punctuated by panic-stricken dashes between refreshment rooms and trains, in terror of leaving someone behind.

As she handed over her charges to the GIS workers and parents waiting on Hamburg station, Joyce, faint from relief and fatigue, needed Margaret's help to keep upright while mothers and fathers filled her arms with flowers. Then she and Margaret were subjected to ordeal by luxury, being put into a sumptuous hotel which, particularly since the refugees were being conducted to a spartan hostel, they could not bear.

Next morning, they moved into a flat shared by two of the guides. It would be their base while they took advantage of unexpectedly being in Germany to visit some camps.

Sue Ryder collected Joyce and Margaret and drove them first to Wentorf, where refugees were "screened" for America. While their "cases" were being considered, eight or nine families were crammed into each noisy, foul-smelling room for weeks or months, with no provision for privacy, apart from blankets slung across on string. Could Joyce and Margaret's civilised young friends really have come from such conditions? It seemed incredible that talented Herkules must have stayed there while his family waited to see if they could emigrate.

Sue then drove Margaret and Joyce over bleak expanses of moor to the prison-like camps from which people came to Wentorf. Each barrack hut housing ten families had evil-smelling corridors, ugly iron stairs and no facilities, apart from a standpipe outside. No wonder the teenagers had raved about "Ockenden's" hot water! Yet their families had lived in comfortable houses in towns and villages before the war.

Each time Joyce and Margaret visited one of "their" children, the parents drew them inside, saying, "Come in! Come in, dear Madame!", generously pressing on them the most lavish meal they could provide. Compelled by politeness to eat food they knew the families themselves must desperately need, Joyce and Margaret found it hard to swallow. Margaret had the added torment of having to eat a double quantity of the strong German sausage she hated, because Joyce, a vegetarian, invariably contrived to slip her portion onto her friend's plate!

Joyce and Margaret found Mirdza and Austra in a small, overcrowded room with rain pouring through the roof. On their return, the sisters had found their father once more in hospital. His tuberculosis had become active just too late for the family to be accepted in a Norwegian scheme to take eighty families whose breadwinners had TB.

That night, as she prayed for a way to help Mirdza and Austra,

Joyce was again guided towards a network of human help. She remembered Anna, the Norwegian teacher who had helped at "Ockenden" that summer and been particularly friendly with Mirdza. Anna's uncle was a leading doctor in Norway. She wrote to Anna to see if her uncle knew about the refugee scheme. Not only did he know about it, he was in charge of it! In no more than a week, Mirdza, Austra and their parents were in Oslo, being given hospitality by Anna's family before being resettled.

Not long after Joyce returned to England, Anna's mother rang in distress to say Anna was ill and confined to a padded cell, with doctors recommending a lobotomy. Begging Anna's mother not to agree to such a drastic operation, Joyce rang the surgery of a Dr Christopher Woodard, whose book, *A Doctor Heals by Faith*, had impressed her. Miraculously, he was already in Norway, attending a conference chaired by Anna's uncle. When his secretary contacted him, Dr Woodard persuaded Anna's doctor, also at the conference, to leave hospital to attend a healing service. One year later, Anna returned to Ockenden healed, having had no operation of any kind.

This network of coincidences led to continuing contact between Dr Woodard and the future Ockenden Venture. Joyce, overwhelmed with admiration for the charismatic, witty doctor, who seemed to have a hot line to God, came to depend upon him emotionally, spiritually and medically. Dr Woodard, though infuriated by Joyce's unpunctuality, multi-faith sympathies and addiction to snappy dogs, was fascinated by her — almost deflected from his life's healing mission, so irresistibly was he drawn into her activities on behalf of refugees. He twice became chairman of The Ockenden Venture.

In 1951 Joyce neither knew Dr Woodard nor guessed that "Ockenden" would ever be more than a conference centre. Yet when Sue Ryder introduced her and Margaret to Muriel Gofton, who was in charge of GIS work in the Hannover–Oldenburg area, and Muriel took them to visit Janina Cichon in Marx camp, "Ockenden's" higher destiny came suddenly nearer. Janina was the tall Polish girl who had taken her precious *Alice in Wonderland* and Polish–Latin grammar book with her to "Ockenden." Her family had been offered hospitality in Kentucky, which they could not accept because Mr Cichon, a former architect, had TB. He and his wife, who was Russian and had been a ballet dancer and actress in Kiev, were deeply uneasy about having to remain in Germany.

Wonderfully, out of their fear and pessimism, grew the solution not only to the Cichon's problems, but also to those of thousands of other refugees in many parts of the world. In an inspired moment, with complete trust in Muriel Gofton, Joyce and Margaret, Janina spontaneously asked if she could live at "Ockenden" and be educated from there.

With alacrity, Margaret and Joyce agreed. Muriel thought the Home Office would give permission, and, though Mr and Mrs Cichon hated the thought of losing Janina, they would not stand in her way. They asked if their other pride and joy, six-year-old Elizabeth or Lala, who was playing barefoot in the sand outside the hut, could go too. It took nine months to obtain visas for the children, which would be renewable as long as they attended school.

6 Vision Extended

Having made the discovery that refugee children would be allowed into England to be educated, Joyce appealed to English schools to offer them hospitality. As a result, when Janina and Lala arrived in June 1952, other girls came with them, looking rather serious after having said goodbye to their parents for a year. One, clutching a white piano accordian passed on to her by a musician who had emigrated from her camp, reminded Joyce of Herkules.

On her way to "Ockenden" with the Cichon sisters was Dace Pavasors, a silent, dark-haired Latvian girl, whose father was a composer and professor of music. He had met Joyce the previous summer in a camp hospital where he was being treated for TB. Five months later, his brother had found his way to "Ockenden" to see her.

"Uncle," a lawyer and author, would one day open a bookshop in the Edgware Road. For the time-being he was working to the best of his ability at the only job he could find, that of an immaculate white-jacketed waiter at The Withies Inn in Compton, near Guildford. "Uncle" told Joyce that his brother and his brother's wife, who was also a musician, were worried about Dace, who, in the course of being transferred from camp to camp, had stopped making progress in music or any other subject. If Joyce would take her to live at "Ockenden" and enable her to have a settled education, "Uncle" would contribute to her maintenance.

Janina, Lala and, more slowly, Dace, became fully acclimatised to life at "Ockenden." Lala, the baby of the group, with her mother's beauty and talent for dancing, was everybody's pet, so enraptured by each new treat that no one could help spoiling her. She longed for a full-length dress, so Joyce bought her a pink crêpe one for her first "Ockenden" Christmas. With her golden hair, let loose from its plaits, rippling down over the dress, she followed a trail all over the house to her present, a wooden pencil box with swivelling compartments.

Joyce was sad but not totally surprised when she heard that the refugees who had gone singly to separate families had felt incapable of living up to their hosts' expectations by appearing happy and grateful all the time. They were returning to the camps. She seized the opportunity to add two of them, Sarmite and Maija Erenpreiss, to her other three at "Ockenden."

Sarmite and Maija's father had owned a bicycle factory in Latvia. Sarmite, or Sarte, described how, after the Russian invasion, their whole family and their old nurse had fled by lorry from Riga to Germany, where they had lived in a cellar before being put into a camp. Though she contracted tuberculosis, Mrs Erenpreiss, Sarte's mother, created an illusion of gracious living in her primitive camp hut in a pine forest.

Since Joyce never discouraged the children from expressing their real feelings, "Ockenden's" atmosphere was not always harmonious. The refugees' underlying worry about their parents and their emotional reaction to a new country aggravated normal family tensions. All the same, it was a healing experience to grow up together. Having similar memories, the children identified strongly with one another, group solidarity giving them the confidence with which to face the world.

Joyce, Margaret and Ruth shared financial responsibility for the five refugees. Joyce, acting as mother, caught all their childhood diseases one by one, giving her own mother the not unwelcome opportunity to walk over to "Ockenden" to exert a nurse's authority.

At the last minute every morning, with Mitch, Joyce's mongrel Airedale racing in front, Joyce and the five children bounded across the park to Greenfield School, which began its tradition of welcoming refugees without charging fees. Once there, though all of them were intelligent, the refugees found it hard to concentrate after their irregular schooling in the camps. Though the younger two fitted into classes of their own age, the others needed coaching from teachers in their spare time. Plans were soon afoot for GCE courses for the older three.

Dace found it hard to relax, looking glum for a long time, hardly speaking, even in German, except to Mitch. Then she surprised everyone with a broad smile. Joyce had the pleasure of taking her shopping, watching her try on a blue dress with which the child had fallen in love when she had seen it in a shop window. It fitted perfectly. At the age of thirteen, Dace's dream of something being bought new, especially for her, had come true.

Dace's new confidence and settled life at "Ockenden" transformed her academic and musical progress. After sixteen months' coaching, she joined the A stream of the Guildford Grammar School, then obtained six O level passes. At about the same time, she played the piano in the London Musical Festival at the Festival Hall.

Joyce continued to hold sixth form conferences. Though their organisation now ran a little late, "Ockenden" was always ready on time on Fridays. The five refugees helped, doubling up in their rooms to make extra space.

During an "Ockenden" weekend in 1954, Dr Christopher Woodard was speaking about absent healing, in which, he said, through the Holy Spirit, power is generated by prayer to heal a sick person. Sensing that somebody was worrying about her father, and finding out from Joyce that it was Dace, Dr Woodard called her over, saying, "If you believe your father can be healed through the power of the Holy Spirit, he will be able to come to Britain."

When Dace wrote to tell her uncle, "Father is definitely coming!", he was furious. How could anyone encourage her to believe something so impossible? Professor Pavasors had recently been desperately ill. As everybody knew, the slightest hint of a recurrence of TB was enough to prevent immigration.

Nevertheless, an exception was made. Dace heard that her father and mother were both being admitted into England. But who would look after her cat in the camp after her parents left? There was no money for quarantine.

Joyce pointed out that it might be just a little unreasonable to expect the Almighty to arrange a passage for the cat too. "I'll pray for him just the same!" said Dace. The following day when she visited her uncle, by chance she met his employer, who, on hearing about her cat, said, "Don't worry. I'll pay for him."

Joyce took the fact that Dace's parents and cat were all coming to England as confirmation that what she and her friends were thinking they must do for all children in the camps, could actually be achieved. Dr Woodard turned to her, at a moment when she was secretly praying for a sign, and said, "Why are you so tense? You have no need to worry. You have everything on your plate. Just go ahead."

After returning from taking the children to Germany for the holiday, Joyce retired for three days' meditation and prayer to a house belonging to her mother overlooking Shoreham harbour. During hours alone on the beach, she thought about the young refugees she had seen still trapped in the camps, surrounded by alcoholism, sexual irresponsibility and degradation. They were likely to become at best apathetic, at worst, delinquent. How could she help them? Could she turn what she was doing for five displaced children into a larger venture?

Confirmation arrived, even before Joyce left Shoreham, in the form of a letter from the bank official in charge of "Grandy" Quartermaine's trust estate. He suggested that she might rent her grandparents' former home, beside Greenfield School, as an annexe for "Ockenden".

Certain now what she should do, Joyce enlisted Margaret and Ruth's help, depending upon them to point out the practical implications of her ideas, relying on them, as she always would, to anchor her vision to reality.

The three decided they would indeed turn the old house into an annexe. They would buy, rather than rent it, so that the restoration work which would have to be done on it would be of permanent benefit.

Once the house had been made structurally sound, Joyce's five "originals" were eager to refurbish it, arguing at the tops of their high, East European voices over what to tackle first — the overgrown, tangled garden or the filthy interior; whether to paint the brown wallpaper or strip it off.

The question of finance remained unsolved.

Joyce called a meeting of everyone who had helped with the original refugees' holiday, announcing her intention to found a charity to bring fifteen more displaced children to Woking. Her family solicitor offered to obtain official charitable status for what would be called The Ockenden Venture, recalling the lovely old house which had first welcomed refugees. Canon Venables of Windsor became the chairman of an Ockenden committee and a register grew of people who would sponsor Ockenden children.

Joyce waited for Maybug, Sue Ryder's car, to be repaired so that she and Sue could set off together to Germany in search of fifteen new children. Their sailing date was finally fixed for January 9th, 1955, but, as Joyce waited on the quay, there was no sign of Sue. Resigned to going alone, and seeing the gangway of their mail boat about to be hauled up, she went on board. At the very last moment, Maybug sped onto the docks and was hoisted up onto the deck by crane.

Ever since the Guide International Service had closed down, Sue had been working in Germany at her own expense, initiating British Army wives into camp welfare work and hurtling along remote, difficult roads in all weathers to visit stateless men who, out of boredom or desperation, had broken the law. Joyce soon found that every day or night journey with Sue was interspersed with visits to prisons.

In Seedorf Camp, a vast area of wooden barracks penning up hundreds of people of varying nationalities, Joyce and Sue found two children who would come to England once they had travel documents. Though a few others would follow later, many parents were too weakened or demoralised to face the thought of losing their children, even if only for a limited period. They depended upon them to do the cooking and were sure that they would never manage without their social security allowances. Some parents were dissuaded from letting their sons or daughters go by neighbours who warned that they might never see the children again. Parents who did accept Joyce's offer considered it an answer to prayer.

Joyce's first night in a DP camp was spent in the Latvian settlement at Ohmstedt, top to toe with Sue in a bed vacated by Frau Lakis, the widow of a former professor of agriculture at Riga University. Frau Lakis had insisted on giving up her bed and going to sleep in a friend's hut. It was snowing heavily as Sue and Joyce ventured out to fetch water to boil on the wood stove in a corner of the room and stumbled along by torchlight to the "toilets", a stench-filled hut of unscreened cattle pens.

The stove generated a suffocating heat inside the hut. Behind a thin partition on the left, a drunken Ukrainian and his wife were quarrelling. Somewhere on the right, a baby cried. Dressing before dawn, Sue slipped out to a camp on the other side of Oldenburg, where she knew there was a child, Halina, whose father might like her to go to England. Meanwhile, Frau Lakis opened her store cupboard, setting out cheese, sardines, tinned fruit and Ryvita biscuits, saved from a Red Cross parcel. She showed Joyce photographs of her former home in Latvia and her collection of books sent by sympathisers in England and America.

While looking for children in Ohmstedt, Joyce found the sister of one who had come on the first Ockenden holiday. Her mother, a graduate, who helped in the camp kindergarten, jumped at the chance of a second daughter's going to England.

In the afternoon, Sue returned to collect Joyce and drive her through the old city of Oldenburg to meet Halina and her father. Five years earlier Halina had watched her mother die from experimental typhus injections in Belsen concentration camp, which was where her parents had met and where Halina had been conceived and born. When Sue and Joyce arrived, the little girl was returning from camp school on her father's bicycle handlebars. She was nervous and sensitive but eagerly opted to join Joyce's group.

Driving through a blizzard to the border of the Russian zone near Helmstedt, Sue and Joyce reached Camp Mariental. Barefoot, shivering children, whose skin was marked with impetigo, ran out in the snow to meet them, hoping for chocolate, though Sue and Joyce had only a few pieces left to give them. Five children in this camp would benefit from English education.

As they crunched along the snowy tracks between the barrack huts, Joyce and Sue heard the jaunty sound of an accordian. Tracking it down to one particular hut, they slipped through the door, into the middle of a Polish wedding celebration and were instantly swept up into a *krakowiak* dance by two young men. Amid all the singing and the toasting of the happy couple, Joyce noticed Sue taking names of children who might come to Ockenden.

The first five children whom "Tante" Ryder brought to "Venture House" in May 1955, reacted with amazement to the baths, the armchairs and the wondrous vacuum cleaner. Otherwise they were quiet and repressed. Joyce's loyal friends, Gordon Maxwell, who owned music shops in Woking, and his wife, Constance, who was prominent in the Inner Wheel, moved into "Venture House" for a month to make the children feel at home. They initiated a happy routine of school, homework, music, ballet and robust indoor games, knitting, dressing puppets, writing letters and making Christmas cards. One little boy, after refusing to speak at all during his first week, planted himself in front of Joyce and said, "I luf you!"

When a second group of children arrived in October, "Venture House" was officially opened by Canon Venables. Colonel and Mrs Rose, the houseparents, and several volunteers who earned only £3 a week, created a happy family atmosphere, amply rewarded by believing that they were providing a permanent solution for DP families. They knew that once the children had been empowered to earn their own livings, they would have the great satisfaction of being able to rehabilitate their parents.

Vague and unconventional though Ockenden's methods of looking after children were, based on a unique blend of intuition, dedication and humility, they worked. Understandably, the children would become depressed and bad-tempered, irritated at having to say "thank you" all the time to people who invited them out and who, for no good reason, possessed so much. They knew they were fortunate to have the chance of education; that one day, if they worked hard, they would be able to earn their own living. That did not always make up for being separated from their parents and for having to forego the wild behavioural freedoms of the camps. Joyce encouraged them to look forward to the holidays as if they were at boarding school. Knowing their parents had not rejected them, they had fewer, less serious problems than children in similar institutions.

All caught Joyce's kindness. One, Stanislav, was spotted wistfully looking at another boy's new toy. A volunteer explained that if Stanislav put aside a small amount from his shilling pocket money, he too would have enough for a toy. The little boy just nodded. On Christmas Day, he handed Joyce a crumpled paper bag containing twenty-one shillings, one for each week he had been in England, saying simply, "To bring someone else from my camp."

All the children were embarrassed about being refugees. When one girl's picture appeared in a newsletter, her friends exclaimed, "Isn't that awful! Look! There she is for everyone to see!" It was hard for them to accept that they should be proud to be triumphing over past, hideous circumstances, over which neither they nor their parents had had any control.

The heart of the Venture remained "Ockenden" where the children ate their meals and where Joyce was, together with an assortment of cats, dogs and rescued fledgling birds. A visitor opening the gate would be met by a loud chorus of ill-mannered barks from Mitch, hysterical yapping from Susan, Margaret Dixon's snappy, ginger mongrel, and the excited yelps of a puppy for whose existence Mitch and Susan were jointly responsible. Then a smiling boy or girl would open the front door, saying, "Please come in! Miss Purse is expecting."

Every summer, Joyce and Ockenden staff drove all round the British zone of Germany, delivering, collecting and visiting children. As Ockenden's family grew, the exodus would one day reach huge coach and train proportions. Dr Woodard and his twin brother, Peter, would be asked to drive cars and minibuses thousands of miles too. For the moment, numbers stayed at twenty. However many broadcasts Joyce made, however many articles she wrote, it seemed impossible to arrange more sponsorships.

"If the need is there," Joyce thought, "there must be a way."

7 The First Great Blossoming

On a foggy, November afternoon in 1955, the hazy forms of Joyce Pearce and Sue Ryder could just be discerned picking their way round a sprawling heap of coke to the arched front door of Donington Hall, a crenallated Midlands mansion.

Over the entrance, below an imposing tower, was a curved stone fanlight filled with heraldic glass, and a carved dedication to Francis, tenth Earl of Huntington. Yet, on that bleak afternoon, no wealthy aristocrat could be found there — only Major Shields, a hard-pressed farmer. In more ways than one, he had been landed with the property. It had been entailed to him, but there was no way he could maintain it as it deserved.

Major Shields had invited Joyce to Donington. After seeing her television appeals, he wondered whether her problems could be solved along with his own. Could Donington be refurbished for refugees?

Major Shields himself, in riding boots and tweeds, opened the door, ushering Joyce and Sue into a wide entrance hall from which a stone staircase spiralled to the cobwebbed shadows of a rib-vaulted ceiling. During the First World War, the Hall, encircled with barbed wire, had been used as a detention centre for German prisoners. After the war, Major Shields's father, its former land agent, had bought it and brought new life into it by refurbishing it, restocking the deer park and laying down a racing circuit which attracted as many as 50,000 people for the Donington Grand Prix. With the outbreak of the Second World War, the staff had five days in which to evacuate the Hall before the Army again moved in, replacing barbed wire, felling trees and erecting Nissen huts, turning the park into one of the largest transport bases in England.

When the Army left in the 1950s, Major Shields returned from East Africa to claim his inheritance. He repaired fences, replenished the sheep and deer herds, installed horses, cleared away the Army's rusty debris and planted new crops and trees. Now, if the Hall itself could be cleaned, it would make an ideal home for large numbers of refugees!

To Major Shields's disappointment, Joyce declined his offer, tantalised though she was by the thought of Donington's fifty rooms. Ockenden's general fund would barely cover clothes and fares for its existing children, let alone refurbish a mock-Gothic hall. In any case, she was fully employed in finding higher education for her "first five" and apprenticeships for older boys whom she had plucked from the improvident, dependent lifestyle of the camps. She pushed Donington to the back of her mind.

There were mountains of paper work connected with The Ockenden Venture: thanking sponsors and benefactors; keeping up contact with families; arranging for new children to replace those who left because parents emigrated or could not do without them. Joyce was becoming a well-known champion of refugees, with meetings to attend in London, talks to give to Women's Institutes and Rotary Clubs, broadcasts and television appearances. She still had her "first five," was still teaching part-time, still organising sixth form conferences, storing all information about refugees in her head, with supporting evidence in hat boxes under her bed or in Sainsbury's cardboard boxes in the boot of her car.

The "first five" affectionately tolerated Joyce's vagueness, even when she cancelled outings she had planned for them, if more important things came along. Half-amused, half-protective, they attended to her appearance like so many theatrical dressers when she had an appointment, making sure her stockings were straight and not laddered, her hemline not dipping, her gloves matching. They had to admit that even when they could not get her to the station on time, the train always seemed to run just late enough for her to catch it!.

On sunny days, she would perch on the window seat, pen in hand, pad on knee, papers littered everywhere. In cold weather, she could generally be found sitting on a low stool by the fire, passports, travel documents and letters making the carpet impassable, except for a few clear patches to step onto. Ignoring the clear patches, Mitch, wet from the garden, would plonk himself down, as near to her as possible.

Into this chaos walked Oonagh, a pretty eighteen-year-old Scottish girl. Visiting her sister, a volunteer cook at "Ockenden," she saw Joyce answering letters in between offering coffee to visitors, supervising children, rushing to emergencies in the kitchen and making up beds for new arrivals. She decided to rescue her.

Though Oonagh could type, she had no professional experience and Joyce had never had a secretary. Their relationship was, therefore, tinged with eccentricity. Joyce still always clutched a bunch of papers in one hand while doing something else with the other. Oonagh, who could imitate Joyce's style in routine correspondence, pursued a moving target to take dictation of more important letters. Driving to Dover with Joyce in a Land Rover full of chattering children, she would be typing away right up to the last moment, jumping out onto the quay just as Joyce was about to drive onto the ferry.

Despite all Joyce's efforts, Ockenden could still support no more than twenty children. Then, in 1956, Russian tanks rolled through the streets of Budapest and 15,000 Hungarians joined the thousands of displaced East Europeans. A powerful surge of sympathy swept them to the front of English consciousness. Joyce knew funds would be raised for them and immigration rules relaxed. What if Donington could become a transit centre for the Hungarians? She might find a way of using it for more long-standing refugees when the Hungarians had been resettled.

To Major Shields's satisfaction, Joyce suggested Donington to the British Hungarian Appeal organisers, who said, "We'll let you know." On her way out of their office, she met the president of the students' union of King's College, London University, going in. "Don't go in there!" Joyce said. "I've got plenty for your students to do. Could you clean Donington Hall for the Hungarians?"

Next morning, "Ockenden's" phone rang. Unlimited numbers of Hungarians were on their way. Joyce called on every available friend and contacted King's College. It took only two days to turn Donington into a hostel. Two hundred students arrived in a fleet of free coaches, armed with gallons of paint donated by ICI, brooms, cloths, ladders and brushes. They worked in shifts, snatching sleep in sleeping bags on the stone floor. Meanwhile, Joyce and Major Shields appealed for furniture and set up a local fund-raising committee.

Hungarian men and boys rolled up, then tumbling crowds of Hungarian families, some with as many as seven children. Janina, Sarte, Dace, Maija and Lala, "poor little Ockendogs", as they called themselves, furious that Joyce had left them behind, made Margaret drive them up to Donington every weekend. The "Ockendogs", Joyce, Margaret and many volunteers slept side by side in camp beds in a room over the hot kitchen, taking turns to silence Mitch's snores by propping up his chin.

Between three and four hundred Hungarians, young and old, peasants and professionals, passed through Donington, people of all sorts living side by side. Joyce stepped between them when they had fights and drove them off to be married when they formed passionate liaisons. Not even she could prevent them lighting camp fires in their rooms if they had not lived in houses before. When the unmistakable smell of wood smoke once again mingled with the rich odour of goulash drifting up from the kitchen and wisps of smoke curled out of a window, she would summon the fire brigade, struggling to keep a straight face as the firemen reacted with shocked incredulity to each new fire.

For two years, Joyce, Rita Comerford (a young volunteer from Woking who was also one of Sue Ryder's secretaries) and Oonagh, combined

Ockenden's office work with correspondence connected with the Hungarians, arranging emigration for many to Canada or Australia, and housing and employment in England for the others. Professional people posed no problem. Factory work was easy to find for Hungarians who could speak English; domestic and agricultural work obtainable for those who could not. By the end of 1958, only one family waited to be resettled. Joyce had returned to "Ockenden." Clean and refurbished, Donington Hall stood empty. Joyce could not raise enough money to fill it with displaced children.

Yet Ockenden was growing. More people were coming forward to sponsor refugees. Seventy-five children were now living in four houses: three houses in Woking ("Ockenden," "Venture House" and "Venables") and "Keffolds," a woodland mansion in Haslemere, supported by a particularly active group of local Friends. "Keffolds" had been vacated by Dr Barnado's from whom Ockenden rented it. Its first housemother, Mrs Cocorda or "Coco", who was Polish, was calm and serene after a lifetime's insecurity and harassment — a soothing presence for uprooted children.

The transportation of large numbers of children to Germany for the summer holiday became a triumph of organisation and endurance, blithely taken for granted by the young refugees. They would sleep hour by hour, in the back of van, minibus or Land Rover, tumbling out to push if it broke down.

Danuta Urbaniec, one of the escorts, could keep the children in order in a confined space but, a refugee herself, she understood why they erupted into naughtiness as soon as they scrambled out of the Land Rover. She fended off uncomprehending criticism in restaurants when the youngsters fought over food. Glaring at German waiters with her steel blue eyes, she would demand to know why young mothers, exhausted and brutalised by slave labour, should be expected to have the will or energy to teach table manners.

1964. A hut in a displaced persons' camp in Germany, from which a child came to Ockenden

Joyce with Christopher Chataway, the athlete and politician, at an Ockenden Open Day

Not even border guards could intimidate Danuta, who was the daughter of a Polish brigadier. When she and Peter Woodard took the children's lovingly gift-wrapped Christmas presents to their families in Germany, she was ordered to open them to prove that they did not contain coffee. She refused to hurry, untying each ribbon slowly and carefully so that she would be able to retie it exactly as it had been before. After she had painstakingly unwrapped and rewrapped the first two parcels, the soldiers impatiently waved the Land Rover through. Peter, in his Father Christmas costume, distributed every present in pristine condition.

Joyce was close to the staff who came and went in the four Ockenden houses, comforting and supporting those who were there because of sadness of their own. Male or female, young, elderly or middle-aged, civil servants, nurses, teachers, secretaries and even unqualified people who had never had a job before, felt needed and inspired to imitate her determination and hard work. The tiny, semi-voluntary office staff watched her non-stop activity in amazement, especially in World Refugee Year, when, as they found their own energy flagging, she slipped into a higher gear.

World Refugee Year (WRY) was launched on the first day of June, 1959, by Sir Harold Gillett, Lord Mayor of London, under the chandeliers of the Mansion House. Gathered together in elegant evening dress, people of all classes, religions and political parties and from thirty-one countries pledged themselves to work to help refugees.

WRY had been proposed in *Crossbow*, the Conservative Bow Group's magazine, following a visit by Timothy Raison MP to Arab refugee settlements in Jordan. Christopher Chataway MP, the famous four-minute miler, whose parents lived in Woking, was also associated with the article. His attention had been focused upon refugees after Joyce had charmed him onto Ockenden's committee. WRY would spotlight the problem, raise money for their relief and encourage governments to relax immigration quotas.

The United Nations Association of Great Britain, whose general secretary, David Ennals MP (now Lord Ennals), was to become a firm supporter of Ockenden, proposed WRY to the UN General Assembly in December 1958. It was accepted and Joyce Pearce and Dr Christopher Woodard (then Ockenden's Chairman) became members of the UK WRY committee.

The British Government pledged a million pounds for WRY, and Britain's voluntary refugee agencies pledged another million, twice their usual annual sum. Two million pounds would resettle 160,000 refugees in Europe and 9,000 Europeans anxious to leave China. It would relieve the Palestinians and assist 800,000 Chinese refugees in Hong Kong.

Amid huge media support and a protracted burst of goodwill, charitable events all over Britain raised five times the target figure. Ockenden's general fund was swollen by £100,000. The Venture received over six hundred new guarantees of sponsorship. Eight more Ockenden houses opened.

A new administrative office was set up in a hut in "Ockenden's" garden. A finance officer, Fred Forty, who had been in charge of Refugee Year finances, was engaged and a professional secretary, Maureen Repassy, left her well-paid position in Shell to work for The Ockenden Venture for a miniscule salary.

With the relaxation of immigration rules, a new Ockenden Family Trust brought some of the children's parents to England. The first couple, the Wojciks, were greeted on Christmas Eve by their three excited daughters in a transit house in Woking decorated with streamers, balloons and a Christmas tree. The children had prepared a traditional Polish Christmas Eve supper of unleavened bread, cold fish in tomato sauce and vegetable salad, creamed potatoes with mushroom sauce and sauerkraut and hot pancakes filled with strawberry jam, to be followed by nuts and coffee.

The Wojciks settled down happily in Haslemere: Mrs Wojcik took a domestic job at "Keffolds" and Mr Wojcik worked on the land. Other Polish parents were less confident. They dared not go out at first, in case they were seized in the street as they had been in their own country. Others were convinced people were hiding in the bushes at night to spy on them and pointing and laughing at them in the street. The friendship and understanding of local English people and the support of their children, who were unusually mature, in the end made them feel at home.

Still, it was hard to balance a budget after years on public assistance. The refugees' wages, which at first seemed colossal, proved unsufficient for the enticing goods displayed in English shops or for the lovely houses most English people seemed to live in. And how could mushrooms, which grew freely around the camp, be so expensive here? Stealing had often been a way of life in the camps. In England, small refugee children in particular were tempted just to take what they wanted.

All over the country, properties were being offered to The Ockenden Venture, the oldest and most beautiful of these being the Hon. David Astor's fourteenth century country house, "The Abbey", at Sutton Courtenay. In medieval times, it had been owned by the Benedictines of nearby Abingdon Abbey and probably used as a place of retirement for invalid monks.

The Polish children who lived there, in beautiful, secluded grounds in the middle of a timbered village, were near a river and dangerously close to a weir but also within reach of the Hon. David Astor's swimming pool which they were allowed to use. Oxford University students invited them to their colleges, provided dance bands for parties at "The Abbey" and arranged punting expeditions.

Joan Leadley, who was in charge at "The Abbey," would have only boys younger than eleven at the same time as Polish teenage girls, for, whichever of the two physical types Polish girls seemed to fall into — tall, dark and slender or short, plump and fair — they were exceptionally attractive. While younger children could easily be moulded into good behaviour, it was harder to influence those who had reached puberty in the camps. When not even Joyce could dissuade one older girl from slipping down to the village at night, the unpalatable decision had to be made to send her home.

Ockenden children reacted very differently to their wide variety of environments. Those at "Hendre Hall," a hotel on the cliffs at Barmouth, loved being beside the sea and close to Snowdon, not objecting to learning Welsh as well as English. On the other hand, the adolescent Polish girls who lived at "Windlehurst," a stone house in Ambleside in the Lake District, liked wearing tight skirts and high heels and longed to be in a town. Open air situations appealed more to boys. At seventeenth century "Bickerton Grange" on the edge of the flat wastes of Marston Moor, Polish boys learned so much about agriculture from their houseparents, the Lovells, a retired farmer and his wife, that many still farm in the area today.

Tom and Pat Lovell, who had four children of their own, had started a new life as Ockenden house parents after a back injury had forced Tom to give up farming. One autumn night they received six Polish children into their isolated Ockenden cottage in Surrey, all frightened and truculent at having had to walk the last mile down the leafy, country lane by torchlight. It had not been the children's idea to come to England. Their seventeen-year-old sister, Irena, an apprentice hairdresser, had written to ask Joyce to take them, after visiting them and their mother in their resettlement flat near Soltan in Germany.

Irena's mother had never known normal adult life. She had been taken for forced labour when she was only sixteen. Unable to cope in her new surroundings, she was drinking heavily. The furniture had been sold to pay debts. The flat was dirty. The windows were broken

Beech Hill House, Reading

Hendre Hall, Barmouth, Wales

Venture House, Woking

Keffolds, Haslemere

Queen Elizabeth the Queen Mother visits Venture House

"The Abbey," Sutton Courtenay, nr Abingdon, Berks

Bickerton Grange, Wetherby

and the electricity had been cut off. When Irena gave her brothers and sisters a meal, they fought even over a boiled potato.

Joyce, who was in Germany at the time, having received a cable about Irena's letter, immediately went to the flat to arrange for the brothers and sisters to have a holiday in England with Tom and Pat. Despite their initial reluctance, the children soon took to their new, ordered life and regular, home–cooked meals and to the Lovell family's assortment of pets. When the Lovells moved to "Bickerton Grange" with their own four children, three white cats, two dogs and a pony, the six Polish were delighted to go too.

At this time, ten Ockenden boys were living in "Westholm" in Birmingham and thirty-seven children and working boys and girls at "Beech Hill," a Georgian house in Reading. Two more Ockenden homes were opened in Woking and The Venture bought "Stoatley Rough," a red–brick mansion in Haslemere, a mile down the lane from "Keffolds" with a magnificent view over the South Downs.

Joyce re–christened "Stoatley Rough" "Quartermaine," after her grandfather. Having already been used as a school for Jewish refugee children during the war, it became an Ockenden school for girls from "Keffolds" and a boarding school for Ockenden boys, acclimatising many to England when they first arrived.

As the "Keffolds" and "Quartermaine" community took shape on the wooded slopes of Haslemere, at "Quartermaine" a miniature farm began to contend with brambles, bracken, burdock and thistles. Hens were moved in and an assortment of run–down, rescued animals, including two seaside donkeys Joyce had seen being ill–treated on a beach. "Miss Elsie" organically tended the kitchen garden at "Keffolds," defying slugs, squirrels, pigeons, mice and deer to produce huge quantities of every type of English fruit and vegetable.

The climax of World Refugee Year for the Woking contingent came in mid–summer, when Queen Elizabeth the Queen Mother spent an informal day with the family. In preparation, staff and children scrubbed and polished the houses and borrowed red carpets from the neighbours. Constance Maxwell persuaded Woking Council to lend sixty red geraniums, setting to work herself in her best dress to dig them into the ground when the man who delivered them at the last minute announced that he could not stay.

Her Majesty, wearing a beautiful, flowery hat, enjoyed herself tremendously, fascinated by the children's stories and Polish dances, and amused and delighted by Joyce from whom she did not want to be parted. "Where has she gone? She's so small, I can't see her," she was heard to say, and made Joyce sit beside her in her Daimler as she was driven between the houses. Every subsequent Christmas a box of royal chocolates arrived addressed to Joyce, tied with a gold ribbon and decorated with a golden tassel.

With the income from WRY and taking advantage of the local goodwill generated by the Hungarians, Joyce could at last use Donington. Its huge bedrooms made ideal dormitories. Other rooms had been converted by the Hungarians into playrooms, workshops, rest rooms and store rooms, a dining room, a sick bay, washing and ironing rooms, a library and a school room.

Yet the first children to live at the cold Hall were miserable, ten miles from the nearest town and two miles even from the village of Castle Donington. The staff were unsettled too, even the Australian housemaster who had worked in boys' clubs all over the world.

"There is nothing else for it," said Joyce to Margaret Dixon. "You will just have to stop teaching and run Donington!"

8 Donington Days

Margaret Dixon arrived at Donington in August 1959. The Polish girls, who hated the Hall so much, sped back to the cosiness of Joyce and Woking, leaving the boys to enjoy the freedom of the country.

There were many ways of keeping warm: chopping wood for the huge fireplaces, playing table tennis and football and riding Major Shields's horses when he was not looking. The Major enjoyed seeing all the activity as he strode around the place, a chiuahua puppy peeping from each of two, deep pockets.

The boys had bicycles and an old motor–bike on which, without any obvious petrol supply, they were somehow able to ride round and round the racing circuit. The mystery was solved when the Hall's ancient taxi, two minibuses and forty–seater bus failed to start.

The open countryside was heaven to the boys after years of restriction in the camps. The older ones who hitch–hiked all over England, took Margaret's advice to trust policemen. Calls were always coming from hundreds of miles away, saying, "We've got your boys. Can you come and collect them?" Since the boys frequently came across bullets left behind by the Army, it was a relief when a local doctor confessed that it was he, not they, who had accidentally shot two of Major Shields's red deer. Margaret took all the live bullets the boys handed over to her to the police station, until the sergeant, becoming bored with them, winked and said, in his slow, Midlands accent, "Now, Miss Dixon, you've a perfectly good well at Donington Hall!"

It was hard to keep track of the boys on Sundays, when there were no lessons to occupy them, and to ensure that they did not sneak away to climb the forbidden ninety–foot battlements or to scrabble about in the cellars to find out which, of many dangerously collapsing secret passages, was the escape route scooped out in 1916 by two German air force officers.

Assuming that one of the 1963 Great Train Robbers who had been stationed at Donington during the war knew about the "impregnable" wall safe in the dungeon, the police borrowed Major Shields's key to unlock the safe in case stolen money had been deposited there. All they found was an empty hole. The boys had long since taken out the bricks from the other side and removed the safe's disappointing contents.

After Margaret arrived at the Hall, ten schoolboys and ten "grown up" apprentices multiplied to eighty at any one time. Three volunteers, Keith, Michael and Shirley, taught them English and general subjects to prepare them for English schools, a handyman tried but failed to teach them carpentry and a Hungarian interpreter acted as matron.

Donington's first cook, who had worked at the Hall in the good old days, hated economy. She lived with her sister, who had also been a maid at the Hall, in Kings Mills, a tiny village down river, where boys tampered with a medieval water wheel and swung over the dangerously swirling water on the fragile, cracking branches of old trees. The meals provided for the refugees by the next cook, who was Hungarian, satisfied their hunger, even though she kept to a firm budget. The third cook cooked only when she felt like it. Finally, efficient Mrs Vynel came in daily from the village and there were no more problems.

Fred Forty, who kept a strict eye on Donington's finances from Woking, was greatly helped by Leicester Education Committee's decision to give the boys free school lunches. Rotary and Inner Wheel clubs provided sports equipment, table tennis tables and a football pitch, and fifty Women's Institutes knitted a red, blue or green "house" jumper for each boy. A silver house cup was presented weekly, full of beer for the older boys and accompanied by sweets for the younger ones. No Polish boy could wait a term for the cup or see the point of a cup's being presented at all, if it was empty.

The seven men who assisted Margaret at Donington believed that, even in a large community, each boy should be treated as an individual.

"Quartermaine," Haslemere

Donington Hall

Ockenden boys at Donington

The "first five" - Maija, Elizabeth (Lala), Samite, Janina and Dace - with Joyce at the Tenth Anniversary Dance

Final Open Day at Donington, 1966. Joyce Pearce, Margaret Dixon and Ruth Hicks

As well as a disco once a term, to which boys invited girls from school, the men introduced thrice–yearly dinners. Younger boys watched enviously as older ones wore suits, used silver cutlery and table napkins, drank wine from the best glasses and were waited on at table. At all other times the boys preferred to wear jeans, changing into them as soon as they were safely out of sight of Donington, piling their grey school trousers in a neat heap under a tree.

One hundred and thirty Yugoslavian, Latvian, Estonian, Lithuanian and Polish boys were educated from Donington. Some attended grammar schools, colleges or universities: others could barely sweep a factory floor. In between were many ordinary boys, some quiet, some full of pranks, some well–read, some musical. Half of the boys settled in England but, as Germany again became prosperous, the rest went home. All had kept in touch with their parents, returning to them without fail every summer holiday.

By 1966, numbers were so low that the boys who remained transferred, either to "The Abbey," Sutton Courtenay, with Margaret and Eric Jones, or to "Beech Hill" in Reading. Major Shields managed to break the entail on Donington Hall and, in 1980, sold it to British Midland Airways.

Today there is no evidence that refugees ever lived at Donington, for, with an investment of one and a half million pounds, British Midland converted the Hall into a sophisticated high-tech centre. Long velour curtains hide the shelves of the old library where, instead of boys struggling to do homework, smartly uniformed men and women tap away on computers, administering flights. On the flagged stone floors, where boys' boots once clattered, deep carpet muffles every sound.

While the boys were at Donington, refugee camps in Germany, as a result of WRY, began to close. Most of the 200 children whom Ockenden staff took home in 1962 for the summer holiday were excited to find their parents resettled in freshly–painted flats with modern plumbing and new furniture. Three boys decided not to return to Ockenden. Since their fathers had found work in the Volkswagen factory at Vorsfelde, there was every chance they too would find apprenticeships.

It was sadder than ever to take home the few children whose parents still lived in camps, for the barrack huts were more desolate than before. Windows were broken, gardens the refugees had planted were overgrown and a musty stench seeped from rotting debris.

Two Keffolds boys belonged to the unluckiest category of refugees who were not being resettled because they lived outside the official camps. In their neat, navy blue Ockenden raincoats, they led Joyce across heathland, along a dusty path hidden by undergrowth, to a broken-down shack in a forest. Geese cackled and bedraggled dogs barked as the boys' six barefoot brothers and sisters ran out to greet them.

Joyce marvelled at the quiet heroism with which parents parted from children, not wanting to upset them, even when they themselves were terminally ill and unlikely to see them again. A Czech mother packed her son's bag, said goodbye cheerfully, then told Joyce, privately, that she was about to have a sixth operation for cancer.

In 1963, when most camps were empty, The Ockenden Venture was at peak capacity. Many of its 600 children were still living in eighteen Ockenden houses, while some had joined parents who had been allowed to come to England. Many children had grown up and returned to Germany. Others, on foreign labour permits, contributed to the British work force as secretaries, sailors, nurses and hairdressers, engineers, mechanics and building apprentices, accountants and caterers.

Now there were no children at "Ockenden." The house continued to be the headquarters of The Ockenden Venture, Joyce lived there and it was Margaret's home base, but its first refugees were leading independent lives. The Ockenden Venture's first period of expansion was at an end.

9 The Plight of Tibet

In October 1972, Ockenden's medieval house, "The Abbey," at Sutton Courtenay, which in the sixties had sheltered Polish children, turned Tibetan for the day to welcome His Holiness the Dalai Lama of Tibet, on his first visit to England. Strong links had been forged between The Ockenden Venture and exiled Tibetan people, for Ockenden had been working with Tibetans for nine years.

Tibetans from all over England, five little handicapped Vietnamese girls and Ockenden staff waited for His Holiness in the drive, clouds of incense wafting around them from *stupas* or stone piles built under the lime trees. Home–made, green and red prayer flags were fluttering from the branches. Banners were strung across the drive, proclaiming "Dalai Lama Zindabad" (Long live the Dalai Lama) and "Welcome to His Holiness." The sacred insignia of lions were traced in white powder on the ground.

After gliding past the stout cooling towers of Didcot, incongruous background to the ancient timbered cottages of nearby Sutton Courtenay, the Dalai Lama's official car approached "The Abbey" between stone entrance pillars draped in green and red hangings with blue and gold designs. Then, accompanied by much bowing and cheering, His Holiness was conducted through the arched Norman doorway, across the courtyard with its wide–branched fig tree, into the house. The only access to the special suite that had been prepared for him was, much to the relief of his security men, up a narrow twisting staircase, askew with age.

The company then assembled in the Great Hall, carpeted for the occasion with Tibetan rugs. A gold–draped throne with a golden cushion had been placed under the minstrels' gallery. From the ballustrade, rows of tiny prayer flags criss-crossed the carved heads of English noblemen on the pannelling beneath. The walls were hung with *thonkas*, ritualistic Tibetan Buddhist banner paintings on silk or canvas, framed with gold brocade. One illustrated the Lord Buddha's parable of harmony — a bird, sitting on a hare, sitting on a monkey, sitting on an elephant.

His Holiness entered the Great Hall in his claret robe worn over an orange undergarment, his broad face lit by a radiant smile. He bowed to everyone present, hands pressed together in a prayer-like attitude, before hanging round everyone's neck a white muslin scarf — sign of peace, purity and respect. Then, seated cross-legged on the throne, one hand upwards in the palm of the other, thumbs gently touching, he led the Tibetans in their sacred mantra,

Om mani Padme Hum (Hail to the Jewel in the Lotus)

each syllable of which is symbolic of one of the divisions of the mandala, the Tibetan wheel of life.

Then His Holiness talked of the religious instinct common to all men. "The repression of this is the enemy of peace," he said. He spoke about the responsibility of the world's peoples for one another's happiness, saying, "All is one. If we learn to understand ourselves, we can identify with the sufferings of others and try to overcome them. Enlightenment comes from loving and serving others, not self, in action springing from heart to heart contact."

His Holiness warned Tibetans not to be distracted from the Path of Enlightenment by Western comforts, but to retain their spiritual and humanitarian values of honesty, kindness and self-control. "Tibet's sun and moon have suffered a great eclipse but one day we will regain our country. The great job ahead now is to preserve our religion and culture."

The solemn part of the meeting over, the Tibetans burst into conversation in the low-beamed dining-room, over a meal of finely shredded vegetables in soy sauce, noodles, momo (tiny balls of dough made from zampa flour and filled with meat and vegetables) and dried cheese. His Holiness, by tradition (which he was to break, twenty years later, when he invited Joyce to lunch) ate on his own. His food had been specially prepared in a separate kitchen.

His Holiness talked eagerly with Tibetan students living at "The Abbey" about how their English qualifications would equip them to help Tibetan people. Tashi Wangdi, who was very serious, and Tsering Wangyal, who was always laughing, were recent economics graduates. Wangdi would become Chief Adviser to His Holiness in Exile. Wangyal would edit *The Tibetan Review*.

His Holiness found it refreshing that Joyce did not treat him like a god. He easily fell into serious conversation with her about practical ways of creating new human understanding. Before he left, he gave her a tiny gold model of Buddha sewn into a golden cloth, only a few of which are given away in any incarnation. He gave Buster, her wheezy old dog, a special blessing.

It was in 1963, when the problem of European displaced people was well on the way to being solved, that Joyce's friend, Jill Buxton, first drew her attention to Tibetan refugees in India, and suggested that Ockenden's expertise could help them.

The Chinese People's Liberation Army crossed the upper Yangze River into Tibet in 1950, determined to obliterate what they called "the darkest feudal serfdom in the world." In 1959, when Tibetans rose up in protest against increasingly cruel Chinese repression, 10,000 were killed in three days. Rather than be a puppet ruler, the Dalai Lama escaped, followed by thousands of his people. His Holiness had such international sympathy that the Indian Parliament greeted news of his safe arrival in India by leaping to their feet in a standing ovation.

Despite their own poverty, Indians welcomed the Tibetans, for the two races had a spiritual affinity. Buddhism had first reached Tibet from India. Risking Chinese anger, the Indian Government allowed His

Holiness to set up headquarters at Mussoorie, a former British hill station, in the pine-covered Sawalik hills above New Delhi. Then Pandit Nehru gave him a property in the Himalayan foothills, at Dharamsala.

At the young age of twenty-eight, surrounded by elderly advisers knowing nothing of the modern world, His Holiness set out to guide his exiled people into the twentieth century. Converting into dollars the gold, silver and antiques he had smuggled into India (1,000 pack animals were needed to carry the articles, though they represented only a tiny fraction of his household treasure), he set up a charitable trust for the rehabilitation of the Tibetans. He wanted them to settle mentally, spiritually, emotionally and physically, and to pass on their heritage to their children. One day the children might return peacefully to Tibet.

There were thousands of unaccompanied children among the exiled Tibetans, whose parents or extended families had been trapped in Tibet or killed in the uprising. Some had perished in the mountain snows or been preyed upon by bears or panthers during their attempted escape, while others had died of grief. Even when they survived, parents had no means of supporting their children. Nomads especially, who spent their lives on horseback tending what remained of their sheep and yaks, could not look after the large numbers of their children who became ill after reaching India. Tibet had been relatively germ-free. Now Tibetan children, living in tents far away from medical care, were suffering from typhoid, tuberculosis, measles, dysentery and polio.

This was before the major influx of help from the world's voluntary agencies and before the creation of large Tibetan settlements in Southern India. The Save the Children Fund had set up some efficient nurseries, the Dalai Lama's sister had created another nursery at Dharamsala and His Holiness The Dalai Lama had set up a Tibetan Homes Foundation at Mussoorie. Yet 4,000 Tibetan children were still homeless.

Jill Buxton had been working as a freelance volunteer in India for two years, nursing, teaching and transporting the sick and handicapped to hospital. Her independent spirit, which had enabled her to carry on her husband's farm single-handed after he was killed in the war, had led her, once her children had grown up, to sell the farm. Using her sister's house as a base, she had made her home a Land Rover. Then she was free to travel the world, doing what she could to alleviate suffering.

Jill had great respect for the Dalai Lama and for what he was trying to do. Taking tea with him in Dharamsala in his bungalow (formerly "Highgrove House", now renamed "The Heavenly Abode"), she told him that Joyce's Ockenden Venture arranged education for refugee children. He was very interested, especially when he heard that care was taken to respect the children's beliefs. He asked if Joyce would come to India to meet the Tibetans.

Joyce's decision for The Ockenden Venture to branch out into Asia was as great a leap in faith as her acceptance of responsibility for European DP children had been. It led her into the heart of the global refugee problem, making the name Ockenden internationally known.

10 Journey to the Tibetans

As Joyce prepared to set out to tour Tibetan settlements, transit centres and nurseries in India, Ruth Hicks and Margaret Dixon were firmly behind her, financially and practically. Ruth would cope with crises in Woking while Joyce was away, as well as running Greenfield School. Margaret would continue doing seventeen jobs in one at Donington. Friends offered to look after Buster — and Joyce's other five dogs!

As she kissed her mother goodbye at Heathrow Airport and Buster was dragged away yelping, Joyce could not help thinking that there was something just a little comic about what she was about to do. What would it be like to meander round a Third World country with another middle-aged lady; sleep in a Land Rover; live on cheese and biscuits to avoid food poisoning and look for a stand-pipe to park beside at night?

She and Jill were to collect Arabella, the Land Rover, from the Sunshine School for the Blind at Lahore in Pakistan where Jill had left it. Their taxi from Lahore airport propelled them along dry, dusty roads through intersecting armies of trishaws and bullock carts, past decaying mansions and sprawling shanty towns. Beggars slumped beside their bowls in the fierce heat and small boys were being dowsed under pumps along with the laundry. Joyce noticed a neatly dressed young man pick something out of a sewer ditch and eat it.

Jet-lagged and shocked by this first encounter with heat and Third World poverty, Joyce fell asleep early on a mattress, on the floor of the blind school, oblivious of lizards darting over the walls and black-striped squirrels playing outside.

Next morning, she wandered into the garden to make friends with the blind children who were playing among vividly-coloured flowers they could not see. Returning inside, she watched more children touching models, trying to understand the reality of trains, cars and bridges.

Though she had come to help Tibetans, Joyce knew her committee, who had changed Ockenden's constitution to allow it to help not just victims of the war in Europe but suffering and oppressed children of any nationality, would stand by her decision to send Margaret Tyson, who ran the blind school, the money for a new classroom.

After stocking up with cheese and biscuits in the bazaar, Jill and Joyce set off in Arabella for the Indian border. The Pakistani customs officer presented Joyce with a pink rose when he heard that she was going to help the Tibetans, and volunteered to explain her mission to the Indian guards on the other side.

As darkness fell, Jill pulled up in a field beside a brick factory. Joyce lowered the back of the Land Rover, banging it shut again as a snarling dog leaped towards it. Lacking Jill's seasoned imperturbability, she twisted and turned all night to the wailing accompaniment of factory sirens and the singing and chanting of brickworkers. When she and Jill opened up the Land Rover next morning, a crowd of women and children had clustered round. They stood staring silently as the two strange English women ate their breakfast of oranges, cheese and biscuits and drank coffee. A row of turbanned men moved across the field scything corn, followed by a row of cows chomping stubble.

Pausing at Amritzar, Jill and Joyce emerged into the light from a barefoot visit to the richly-patterned interior of the Golden Temple. Outside, in the muddy waters of the lake, around which garlands of golden marigolds were heaped on stalls or hung on the branches of acacia trees, sick Hindus were being immersed, seeking healing. "How similar the needs and hopes of all human beings are!" Joyce thought.

Later that morning, she and Jill met two more Indians hoping for cures. A man with toothache and a woman with neuralgia stepped out of a small crowd waiting at the traffic gate where the road became one way, to see if the English women had medicines. Jill handed each of them two aspirins, giving two more to a boy who asked if he could take some for his mother.

Rising above the dusty plain, the road spiralled between slopes purple and red with trees towards the snow-capped Himalayas. Jill stopped at a half-way gate, where two starving dogs greedily gulped down biscuits she and Joyce gave them. A Hindu bridegroom, resplendent in gold jacket and jewelled turban, was carried across the road, sitting cross-legged on a litter, followed in prancing procession by several male relatives.

Night was beginning to fall as, leaving other motorised traffic behind, Jill and Joyce overtook groups of nomads on the move from plains to mountains for the summer. The women, who wore rings in their noses, were balancing food and cooking utensils on their heads and swinging nets of brass pots. The men were driving cattle and carrying bales of straw. Groups who had stopped for the night, lit fires and settled down to sleep on the road, were surprisingly good-natured about being disturbed.

The glare of the Land Rover's lights round a sharp, upward bend sent a buffalo toppling over a precipice. Taking one hand off the steering wheel, Jill grabbed Joyce to stop her jumping out after the animal, which fortunately must have landed on a ledge. As they looked back, they could see a pair of horns jerkily reappearing.

At last Jill and Joyce reached Dalhousie hill station to which hundreds of Tibetans had been transferred. The air was cool and fresh. Joyce locked the shutter against marauding wild creatures before bedding down behind Jill among spare tyres, tea chests, tins and water bottles and cardboard boxes full of baby food.

Next morning, before visiting Dalhousie, Jill drove through dense forest along a rough road passable only in summer, across a swinging bridge with prayer flags fluttering to a hospital at 8,000 feet. She wanted to check that Nawang Chota, a young Tibetan for whose nursing training she had paid, had finished his course. The hospital's Indian doctor pointed out his X-ray apparatus and showed off his TB ward, of which he was very proud, saying that, at a hospital down the road, operations were still being performed outside under the trees. Joyce promised to tell UNICEF that the doctor also needed a mobile X-ray unit to use in the villages in the 2,000 square mile area for which he was responsible.

Having returned to Dalhousie and parked in the market place, Jill and Joyce scrambled on foot up a switchback track to Kailesh boarding school for the élite of Tibetan boys. The boys, whose status as incarnate lamas had been confirmed by the Dalai Lama, were being trained to become spiritual leaders, of whom the Tibetans had great need. Only 7,000 out of 600,000 monks, together with a few hundred lamas, had escaped from Tibet, many of whom had since succumbed to disease and death. Most of those who had been left behind had been defrocked, their monasteries gutted by the Chinese. The little lamas would give Joyce an idea of what standards could be achieved by all Tibetan children. However holy they might become, at present they were as mischievous as any other Tibetan boys.

It seemed incredible, giving rise to the usual exclamations of how small the world is, that Mrs Freda Bedi, who ran this school for lamas high up in the mountains in North West India, had attended the same Derby grammar school as Margaret Dixon. After marrying a Punjabi, a fellow Oxford graduate, she had gone to live in India, obtained a high post in the Indian Civil Service and been put in charge of a transit centre for Tibetans. She now devoted her life to helping Tibetans preserve their culture, assisted by lama teachers, Tibetan assistants and four Western volunteers — two young Englishmen, a Norwegian in a turban and an American girl who had hitch-hiked there from Tangier.

In addition to book learning, the young lamas' education included trips in buses lent by the Upper Punjab Government, to factories, welfare projects and community centres, in order to acclimatize them to the modern world. In spite of Government help, there was a shortfall in funding. Joyce promised that Ockenden would fund sponsorships for some of the boys.

Jill led the way down the mountain to Arabella, striding along to keep warm, with Joyce in her high heels following more slowly. Neither knew, until afterwards, that someone had seen a bear prowling in the nearby forest.

Next morning, Joyce walked up the mountain again to interview older boys whom the Dalai Lama had suggested might train as teachers and administrators in England. She determined to bring one or two to Ockenden by the end of the year — they were so desperate to have higher education.

So that Joyce could seek official sanction from the Indian Government for Ockenden's plans, Jill drove her downhill, round ninety degree bends, to the straight 250-mile main road to Delhi. There she obeyed the instruction to "Horn please!" on the back of every flower-painted silver lorry, while Joyce photographed camels turning water-wheels and red-necked vultures clustered on carcases of cows or crouched, round-shouldered, in leafless trees.

Jill, who preferred sleeping in Arabella, even in the middle of Delhi, installed Joyce in a new hostel attached to a Buddhist temple, lending her a primus stove to make tea. Next morning, they were allowed through the main gates of the Government buildings to deliver a note to the house of Pandit Nehru. Mrs Indira Gandhi (who was not, as yet, Prime Minister of India, but stewardess of her father's household until he died the following year) telephoned next morning to give them an appointment. Receiving them in a wood-panelled, blue-carpeted office, overlooking lawns, fountains and rose gardens, she listened appreciatively to their plans. She asked them to write everything down, promising to do everything she could to help.

Struggling on through Dehli's heat and dust storms, Joyce obtained a guarantee from the Indian Government of 60 rupees a month for every Ockenden Tibetan child, and the assurance that food, medical equipment, footwear and clothing sent by Ockenden to the Tibetans would be exempt from customs duties and transported free from ports. She arranged for the Chartered Bank to deal with Ockenden's financial transactions and for the World Council of Churches to administer the Homes' funds. Then she met a wide network of Jill's friends — artists, philosophers, welfare workers and idealists — and gave a talk, arranged by Jill, to the Service Civil International group at the Delhi YWCA.

Joyce's keenness to help Tibetans did not blind her to the needs of destitute Indians, any more than it had prevented her from helping the Blind School in Pakistan. When Jill took her to visit a home for beggars and handicapped people in a stony, derelict part of Delhi, she promised to send the young man who ran it, who had only a law degree, some trained nursing volunteers. Marvelling at the extent of Jill's knowledge of welfare projects in India, she accompanied her to take an old lady to a Cheshire Home at Kalkaji, a wild, isolated place, where buffaloes were bathing in a pool of stagnant, scummy water.

Now, at last, it was time to continue the fact-finding tour, beginning with the Dalai Lama's Tibetan Homes Foundation at Mussoorie. This entailed another overnight in Arabella, during which Jill and Joyce fed biscuits by moonlight to a passing herd of elephants. The road wound up a horse-shoe shaped cleft in the mountains, from the rim of which deep, wooded gorges sloped down to the Jumna river. The hillsides of Mussoorie, dotted with large, white houses, surrounded by oak trees, firs and rhododendron bushes, made Joyce think of Haslemere. It was a thriving tourist town with a panoramic view of mountain peaks.

On the edge of Mussoorie in Happy Valley (not a valley at all, but a hillside village), Jill parked Arabella outside a dignified, new Tibetan High School whose headmaster was Mr Jigme Taring, future Education Director of the Tibetans in Exile. His wife, Mary, small, neat and dark-haired like most Tibetan women, wearing a traditional, long, horizontally-patterned apron, welcomed Jill and Joyce inside.

Rinchen Dolma Taring (Mary to her English friends) was a member of Tibet's aristocracy, for her mother was descended from the tenth Dalai Lama and her father had been Prime Minister of Tibet. She herself had been the first Tibetan girl to have a Western education in Darjeeling, at Mount Hermon, an American Methodist school. Her husband, Jigme, Prince of Taring, son of Taring Raja of Sikkim, had been the first Western-educated Tibetan boy.

The Dalai Lama had enlisted Mr and Mrs Taring as teachers for the exiled Tibetan children, sending Mary to Lucknow to learn the latest methods. More recently, he had put her in charge of the Tibetan Homes Foundation, which he financed himself from his own funds with assistance from the Indian Government.

Mary and Jigme Taring took a parental interest in the exiled children, passing on Buddhist teachings of peace and love, explaining again and again what had happened and why they were in India. They told them they were responsible for maintaining, and for taking back to Tibet, the Tibetan way of life.

Having been cut off from her own children and grandchildren by fire and bloodshed in Lhasa, Mary knew how the bereaved Homes' children felt. She warmed to Joyce immediately, detecting her sympathetic understanding of the orphans' needs. After serving Jill and Joyce Tibetan tea, with salt and rich yak's butter, she took them to one of the Homes, a former British mansion from whose roof Tibetan prayer flags were fluttering.

Seeing Mrs Taring, Joyce and Jill approaching, children working in the Home's small vegetable and flower garden downed tools and danced in a circle, singing a welcome. "There is no activity for which Tibetans, even in exile, will not spontaneously compose a song," commented Mrs Taring happily.

The Home's *amala* (mother) and *pala* (father), Mr and Mrs Tundra, had created a Tibetan atmosphere with articles of their own which, since they had been intending to move to Kashmir, they had fortuitously packed up before the uprising. As Jill and Joyce drank more Tibetan tea, this time from Tibetan cups with silver stands, they were introduced to the Tundras' two Tibetan dogs. Mrs Tundra told them that a third dog had been eaten by a leopard.

Small, round Tibetan children sitting on low tables in the Home's dining room, doing homework, knitting or sewing, jumped up and clustered round to be hugged, tugging Joyce and Jill to see their clean dormitory with its new beds and bed covers and the prayer room, with draped altar and wood-burning stove. They pointed out a carved orange throne on which the Dalai Lama had sat when he had officially opened the Home. It had an orange cushion which Mr Tundra had made out of his own robe.

The children's day began with bed-making and room tidying at 6.30 a.m., then all except the cooks for the day gathered for prayers and the Tibetan national anthem. Sitting cross-legged on low seats, they were served tea, bread and bulgar wheat porridge which they ate after chanting a grace. Having washed the dishes, they dashed off to school.

Keen for The Ockenden Venture to rent similar houses for the Homes Foundation, Joyce and Jill walked with Mrs Taring to look over two adjacent properties above a rocky track called Dick Road. "Silverwood," the smaller house, had a landscaped garden with a fountain. The other, a white-washed villa, had a stupendous mountain view. Joyce decided to rent the larger house, for which transaction, to the amusement of agent and landlord, Mr Taring insisted an agreement should be typed out. The signing ceremony took place in a tiny room in the Library Bazaar, above shelves of lurid paperbacks.

Mrs Taring told Joyce that Happy Valley urgently needed medical help. She had equipped a small infirmary in which, thanks to the work of an English nurse, no children suffering from measles had died, though forty children had died of measles at Dharamsala. Now the nurse herself was in hospital, having collapsed from exhaustion. There was no qualified person to replace her and a visiting Japanese doctor had found four untreated cases of pneumonia in the infirmary. Joyce promised to tell UNHCR

Jill and Joyce's first stop, after Happy Valley, was at 6,400 feet, at the Service Civil International nursery at Kasauli hill station. Fifty or so sickly, dirty babies were being spoon-fed grated cabbage, beans, rice and cheese on a verandah, then they were laid down, two to a box, to sleep.

After a restless night, with thunder and lightning crackling and crashing on the peaks around, Jill negotiated a rushing stream of a road to a school at Chota Simla, where ragged children, who in Tibet would have been learning traditional crop cultivation, stock breeding or crafts, were tackling academic subjects. The first headmaster having committed suicide and the second having resigned, a schools' inspector had decided to sort out the situation himself. The children returned Joyce's smiles but she noted down their need for more teachers and a matron.

"Stirling Castle," a Save the Children Fund home for Tibetans which Jill took Joyce to see in Simla, though not as warmly Tibetan as the Homes in Happy Valley, was spotless and airy, with light blue paintwork and, in contrast with the boxes into which babies were put at Kasauli, a bed for every child. Learning that the beds cost only fifty rupees a pair, Joyce sent word that Ockenden would pay for as many beds of this type as were needed in the Kasauli nursery.

Two hundred gruelling miles further on, along a rough mountain road, Jill and Joyce reached a Tibetan monastery at Rawalsaw. There, it was said, the guru Padna Sambhare had saved himself from burning by changing fire into a lake on which he himself was sitting in the centre of a lotus flower. Joyce was upset to see children, who were obviously starving, swarm into the lake to pick out pieces of bread she had thrown to some carp. Standing beside the water, watching wistfully, was a woman carrying a child too weak to stand. Joyce gave the mother what was left of the Farex with which she often made meals for herself in India.

It was all the harder, after that, to eat rice, meat, sliced tomatoes, onions and cucumbers which the monks, in spite of their poverty, had prepared for their English guests. Joyce promised to take word to Delhi that this colony of Tibetans had been bypassed in the allocation of basic rations.

Before leaving Rawalsaw, Joyce was taken into a building above the dak (guest house) to meet a young, orange and red-robed incarnate lama. He was enthroned beside an altar laden with silver incense cups and holy pictures, including one of His Holiness the Dalai Lama. He and his guru each presented Joyce with a white scarf. Then, to her surprise, the lama put his arm around her neck.

Nearer Dharamsala, twisting through a gorge covered with pine and cedar trees to the green meadows of the Kullu valley, Jill and Joyce came upon a group of weather-beaten elderly Tibetans. They were employed in heavy digging and earth-moving, to repair the road after the ravages of the winter snow — the only work India, with unemployment problems of her own, could provide for them. They were cheerful enough, though at home they had probably been landowners, farmers and shepherds. Their tents, though not woven from Yaks' wool as tents were in Tibet, were strong, waterproof, ex-army models.

In rocky landscape overlooking the Ban Ganga torrent at Kanga, Joyce found forty Tibetan boys and girls crammed into a small transit centre in which, while she had been in India, forty-eight children had died. That evening, twenty-four more starving children arrived, having had nothing to eat for the last five of many days it had taken to travel from a transit camp at Pathenkot. Food was quickly prepared but there were no spare beds for the children. As they sat and wept, cross-legged on the floor, with Joyce sitting beside them trying to comfort them, one had an epileptic fit from terror.

Shocking as the sight of the transit centre at Kanga was, its conditions were luxurious compared with those in the overcrowded Tibetan school in Lower Dharamsala which Jill and Joyce visited next. There, two hundred children, suffering from dysentery, worms, conjunctivitis and typhoid fever slept one on top of each other on a small verandah. The only sanitary precaution was the rule that water should be taken from above a line of stones in a nearby stream for drinking and from below the line of stones for washing.

Jill brought out medical supplies from the van, for the school had none at all, then set about teaching boys to build camp latrines. Joyce planned to tell the Indian authorities about this institution too, so that basic rations could be sent.

At this point two Tibetan boys asked to borrow the key to start "their" Land Rover. Jill said, "You don't really need the key. Look!" and proceeded to demonstrate with a piece of wire. Three hours later, a mechanic was still at work!

There were already 800 children in the Dalai Lama's sister's nursery in Dharamsala, which had been intended for just 300. With only one hour's water supply a day, they could not be kept clean, nor could the depressing stench be expelled from the grim buildings. Children swarmed round Jill while she unloaded clothes, medicines and tinned food. Others, too ill to notice, wandered round the compound, heads bent, hands to eyes, unable to bear the light. All were suffering from inflamed gums because of a deficiency of vitamin C. They needed tonics, iron and cod liver oil.

The small Dharamsala children, itching with heat and bed bugs, slept six and seven across single beds. In addition to their physical discomfort, they had deep emotional wounds yet there was no one to give them the attention they needed. Loving and conscientious as the Tibetan ayahs were, there was only one of them to every twenty-five orphans. Even more inconsolable than the orphans were children whose parents had brought them to the nursery on the assumption that His Holiness's sister would know more than they themselves did about bringing up children in India. The abandoned children hurled themselves again and again at the locked door.

After an exhausting, saddening tour, it was a great relief to be welcomed with simple courtesy into His Holiness the Dalai Lama's summer "palace" (actually a tin-roofed British-built bungalow on the side of a mountain) and given Tibetan tea.

His Holiness faced his country's troubles with serenity. If you can do something about a tragedy, he believed, there is no reason to agonise over it. If nothing can be done, there is, after all, no point in agonising. To look on the bright side, being expelled from Tibet had given his people the impetus to modernise their society. When they returned home, they would take with them a new constitution, based upon the teachings of Buddha but also influenced by the Universal Declaration of Human Rights.

His Holiness was grateful to Joyce for having written such a detailed report for UNHCR. Many foreigners had tried to help Tibetans but had failed, through ignorance. He laughed delightedly when Jill produced wool and knitting needles to show him she was still knitting red socks for lamas.

11 Tibetan Venture

Back in England, with the exquisite timing of Providence (something to which Joyce was becoming accustomed), a new friend materialised who was to be dramatically effective in publicising the plight of Tibetan orphans. This was the internationally-known actress, Ingrid Bergman, whose part in *The Inn of the Sixth Happiness*, a film about Gladys Aylward's work for young refugees, had made her long to help child victims of war. Miss Bergman had flown to Formosa to meet Miss Aylward, only to find on arrival that, just two days earlier, the "small woman" had died.

During a run of *A Month in the Country* at the newly opened Yvonne Arnaud Theatre in Guildford, Miss Bergman heard about Joyce and sought her out. She liked her at once. For the rest of her life she was often to be found hugging children in Ockenden houses. Her first radio appeal for all Ockenden's children resulted in donations of £11,000 and in listeners writing in from all over Britain to sponsor Tibetan children.

An Ockenden Venture committee member, Miss Kathleen Goldie-Smith, used an inheritance to buy the house Joyce had rented (now called "The House of Faith") for the Tibetan Homes Foundation and the Hon. David Astor rented "Silverwood." As a result of Joyce's report to UNHCR, the American Emergency Committee for Tibetan Relief furnished the houses, provided nursing staff for Mrs Taring's clinic and set up two small, well-equipped hospitals.

Just one month after Joyce returned to England, Jill Buxton drove the first vanload of sore-covered children to the "House of Faith" in Mussoorie, from whose roof, as from the roofs of all the Tibetan homes, prayer flags were fluttering. Mrs Taring wrote to Joyce, "I am happy to tell you that fifty children have gone into your English house. They were so thrilled to see their new home, their new beds and sheets, and the houseparents so eager to receive them. After their rest, they were all given hot baths and then put to bed after a hot cup of milk."

Older children from "The House of Faith" attended Mr Taring's High School and Ockenden volunteers, Valerie Swinscoe and Susan Headley, went to Happy Valley to run a kindergarten. Vitamins and multi-purpose foods supplemented a diet of rice, dal and vegetables, meat once a week and eggs and fruit twice weekly. The children regained health and roundness, jumping and running about as if they had never been enfeebled. In the afternoon, they tended the garden and learned how to make Tibetan boots, scrolls and plaques and the girls were taught dancing and singing by their house parents. Older children constructed assault courses in the trees, explored the wooded gorges and climbed boldly up to the bare, wind-swept ridges.

In December, Mrs Taring, with the help of Valerie and Susan, organised the first English-style Christmas party in a hall decorated with streamers, surprising the house parents as much as the boys and girls. During Pass the Parcel, the Tibetan children thought the paper and string were the prizes and put them into their pockets. The real prize was a Tibetan comb. Ockenden tea chests had arrived just in time, full of blouses and jumpers for the girls, jumpers and shorts for the boys and presents for everyone. Having gone up to receive his gift from Mrs Taring, each child sat down thrilled, not guessing that the lovely Christmas wrapping had to be torn off.

In the Spring of 1965, Yangzom, an almond-eyed girl of seven or eight, nicknamed "Little Nightingale" because of her sweet singing voice, began to complain of head pains, and to stagger sideways instead of walking. She ceased to be able to use her hands or focus her eyes. Peter Woodard, Ockenden's India representative, who loved making the Tibetan children laugh with his pidgin Tibetan or by producing a toy mouse from nowhere or giving them his monocle to try, was shocked by her condition. Against all advice, on his own initiative, he arranged for her to be admitted to the Great Ormond Street Children's Hospital in London.

The Ockenden Venture and the Save the Children Fund paid Yangzom's fare and Valerie Swinscoe travelled to England with her. Peter, and everyone else who knew Yangzom, prayed. Peter's faith was justified. Surgeons at Great Ormond Street, operating without charge, successfully inserted a valve into the little girl's brain to draw away permanently the fluid that had been causing pressure on it. After some weeks' convalescence at "Ockenden", Yangzom could walk sturdily again, enjoyed writing and drawing and was cheerfully looking forward to going home.

When "Silverwood's" lease ended in 1965, "The House of Faith" was extended. Then in 1966, when help for Tibetans became a joint European project, Swiss Aid took financial responsibility for fifty of the seventy-five children. Ockenden opened a school for the artistically-gifted in Happy Valley, with a Tibetan artist as teacher.

Joyce, who often visited Mussoorie, went there in February 1971 with Dr Christopher Woodard. After being welcomed as members of the family at the wedding of Tashi Topyal and Genyen Choeden, who had both lived in the Ockenden community in England, she and Dr Woodard watched new prayer flags being hoisted on the prayer hill for Losar, the Tibetan New Year. As Tibetan trumpets blared across distant peaks, rice was hurled into the air as a sign of good fortune. Joyce and Dr Woodard joined in the children's three days of traditional dancing and drama.

As numbers at "The House of Faith" increased to 145, Ockenden paid for the house's refurbishment and for tiers of bunks to be installed. Today the home is as crowded as ever. Even as children grow up and move out, more children are smuggled out of Tibet and brought to the Homes Foundation, which still depends upon international support from organisations such as Ockenden.

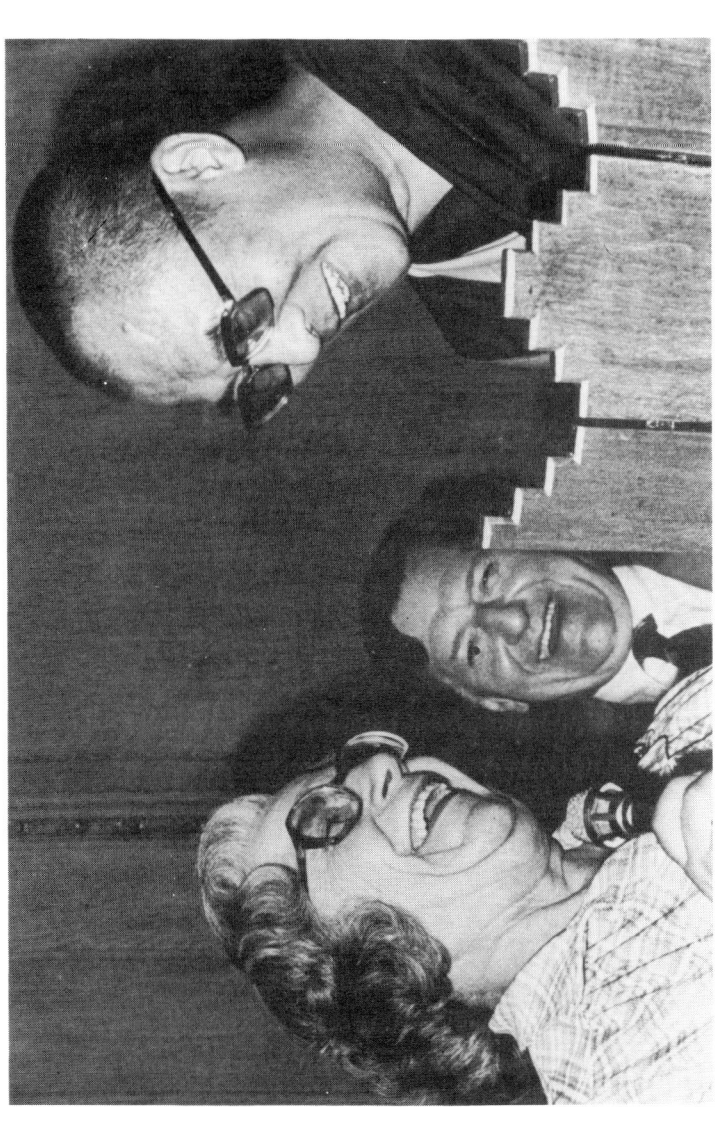

Joyce Pearce with Lord Ennals and His Holiness the Dalai Lama 1984. Courtesy Bill Beminster

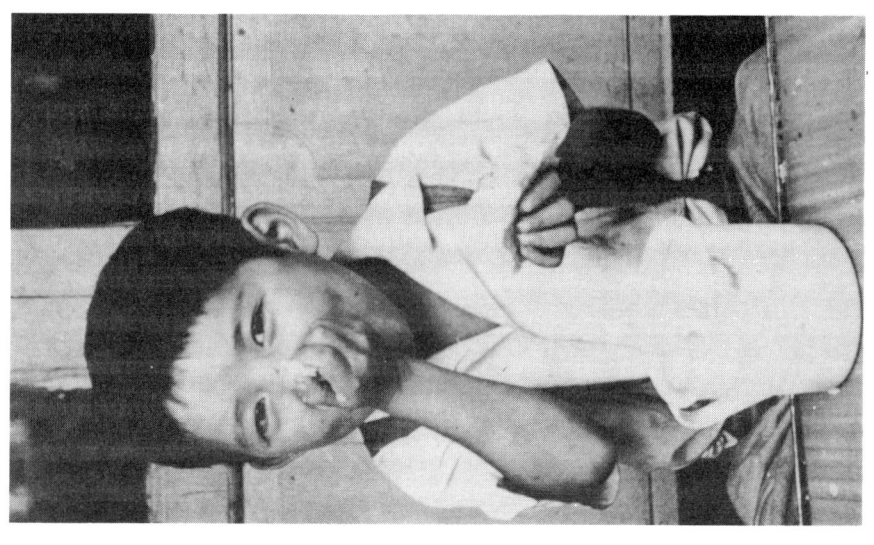

A Tibetan boy in Mussoorie

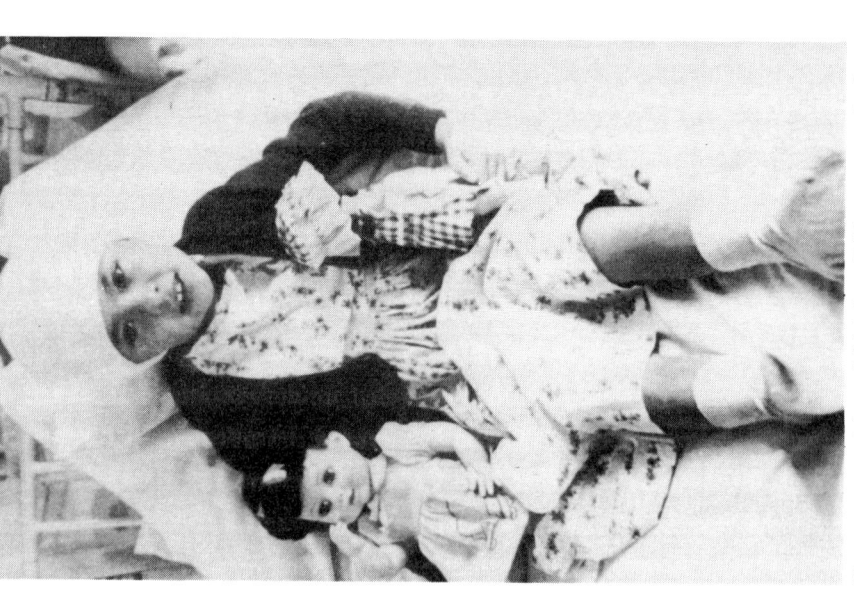

Yangzom, the little Tibetan girl saved by the surgeons at the Hospital for Sick Children, Great Ormond Street, London

Susan Spencer with Tibetan children of the Kindergarten, Happy Valley, Mussoorie

The House of Faith, Mussoorie

Tashi Topgyal and Genyen Choeden, two former Ockenden students married in Mussoorie, India, February 1971, with Mr and Mrs Taring, Dr Woodard and Joyce Pearce

In spite of the careful research and preparation that went into all projects Joyce initiated, it was no simple matter to organise them from thousands of miles away. Two training centres for Tibetans in India, on which Joyce and others expended enormous physical and emotional energy, after working well at first, foundered because of factors beyond Ockenden's control.

One of these centres, an Ockenden Venture training project for Tibetans in Uttar Pradesh, succeeded for several years. Joyce had initially been asked to set it up by the feudal leader of 150 Amdo Tibetan families. The Indian Government had given the Amdos a hundred fertile acres at Clement Town, on which they had pitched tents, built huts and cleared land. They now needed training in building, agriculture, business and light industry.

In 1965, having secured funding from Oxfam, Swiss Aid to Tibetans, The Canadian Refugee Aid Society and Norwegian Aid, Joyce appointed Toby Gooch, a young Tibetan–speaking Englishman with a degree in overseas social administration, to open a basic skills training centre. Two volunteers, Phyllida Sturdy and Carol Bowyer, also went to Clement Town to open a primary school and a kindergarten for Amdo children, for which books, puzzles and games were donated by local families. Money for benches, blackboards, tables and teaching aids was raised at far–away English coffee mornings.

While classrooms were still under construction, practical courses were started in existing industrial units, the most over–subscribed being car mechanics using a second–hand Jeep, an Austin car and an ancient tractor (also hired out to local farmers). The whole community benefited from the centre. Agricultural students ploughed the land and grew wheat, vegetables and fruit; bricklaying students erected neat rows of houses; carpentry students constructed doors and windows and commercial students helped run small businesses such as the manufacture of Tibetan bells and temple horns, in people's homes.

Then came the first bombshell. The Indian Government had such severe unemployment problems that it revoked permission for the employment of foreigners, which affected Ockenden as well as other organisations. Toby and Phyllida packed up and left, followed by Carol, after she had trained a kindergarten teacher. Ockenden appointed a retired Indian army officer, Major Sant Ram, as director, responsible to the existing education committee, whose chairman, John Martyn, formerly headmaster of the famous Doon School, was now Ockenden's representative in India.

In 1972 the Clement Town training centre was still flourishing. Joyce and Dr Woodard presented certificates to the course's many graduates who were finding it easy to obtain work.

Then disturbing reports from John Martyn reached Woking. The Amdos were irritated. The Clement Town centre, the only basic skills training centre for Tibetans in the whole of India, attracted more Tibetans from outside than from inside the Amdo community, yet it was taking up much of the Amdos' precious land. Moreover local jobs were going to graduates of the training school, who tended not to be Amdos.

The final blow came when Swiss and Canadian Aid withdrew financial support from the training centre because of the way some of their other grants to Amdos were being used. Debts mounted. Shopkeepers began to pound on Major Sant Ram's door.

Despite having a broken arm and a sick finance officer, Joyce embarked on a rescue operation, flying to Geneva to address UNHCR, appealing to the British Standing Conference for Refugees and coaxing bridging loans from Norwegian Aid and Oxfam. She pledged £3,000 from Ockenden, on condition that the training centre could reopen within three months. Unfortunately, by this time, such bitterness had developed between the leader of the Amdos and Major Sant Ram that a quick resurrection was impossible. The unique training centre had to be abandoned.

This setback was not allowed to interrupt Ockenden's association with Tibetans. On the contrary, widening its scope, the Venture contributed to a home for Tibetan elderly, provided a clean water supply for a Tibetan settlement of 4,500 people, injected capital into an Tibetan agricultural cooperative in Arunanchal Pradesh and set up a primary health care programme for a community of 900 Tibetans. A few young, handicapped Tibetans came to live with Ockenden in England, under Britain's agreement to admit ten or more handicapped refugees every year.

Ten-year-old Ngawang Thondup, who was deaf and dumb, was found by the roadside and brought to Joyce by Jill Buxton for care, special education and skills training under the guidance of Rosemary Pickering in Woking. Several years later, when he was grown up, Ngawang was taken to Dharamsala for a holiday and recognised by someone who had come from the same village as he in Tibet. Reunited with his family, he burst into tears on recognising his astonished and delighted mother. He stayed on in Dharamsala for several weeks before returning to vocational training in England.

Another of many handicapped Tibetans given special treatment in England by Ockenden was Tsering Gombo, who had escaped from Tibet, aged eight, on the back of a yak. His extended nomadic family had begun imperceptibly shifting their flocks from 18,000 feet up in the mountains in north-west Tibet, after his grandmother had been beaten up by the Chinese for something she had said at a "re-education" meeting.

The flight took a whole year, the nomads moving from one grazing ground to another, sometimes higher, sometimes lower, but always nearer to India. A few went ahead to find a route over the mountains, followed by children and wives on yaks and horses. Most men lingered behind, pretending the women had gone higher up only to feed the animals.

The winter was so severe and the passes so high that, by the time the nomads struggled down into dry, barren Laddakh, of all their huge herds only one yak and two goats were still standing. Now they themselves began to succumb to disease, the dead deprived even of a peaceful grave, as corpses buried in the shallow, hard-baked soil were ripped out by dogs in the night.

Polio which killed his younger brother, paralysed Tsering's legs. When his parents resumed their nomadic life, they were forced to leave him behind. His grandmother took him to a settlement in Muncot, where Jill Buxton met him. Jill found a doctor in Delhi who could help Tsering and later paid his fare to London. Aged fifteen, trundled into Gatwick Airport arrivals hall in a trolley, unable to say more about his destination than "school," Tsering saw Joyce dashing up late to collect him, closely followed by her little Polish foster daughter, in bright red gum boots, and the panting Buster. Jill paid for Tsering to have further medical treatment, attend Langley Court Preparatory School, King Edward's School, Witley, and, lastly, Guildford Technical College. Then he was equipped to earn his living.

Tsering always hoped that one day he would find his parents. In 1982, after six months' search in India, followed by a trek by truck and on horse-back over the mountains, he made contact with his nomadic family at a trading post where, for three weeks every year, they bartered wool for everything they needed. His parents, who were colourfully dressed and had long, black pigtails, had had more children and built up new goat and yak herds. They were overcome with joy at seeing their eldest son whom they had assumed was dead.

Tsering, by now thoroughly Westernised, regarded Ockenden as his home. Yet from that time on he kept in touch with his extended family, discovering more and more of them, in Switzerland and in America, as well as in India.

In 1982, Ockenden opened a Tibetan Cultural Centre in Glisson

Road, Cambridge, where Tibetans and others could learn about Tibet. Yeshe Tsultrim, its administrator, encouraged people of all nationalities to share ideas there, different faiths operating side by side to achieve peace of mind. Joyce and His Holiness the Dalai Lama hoped that Tibetans, who had come to terms with their terrible suffering, could demonstrate that it is possible to overcome anger and bitterness.

On the 26th anniversary of the Lhasa uprising, Independence Day, 23rd March 1985, it was to the Tibet and Tibetans in Britain Societies in London that Joyce delivered her last address. She spoke about the achievements of Tibetans in exile. Since 1963, when she had first found them, shocked, sick and poverty-stricken in India, they had created a democratic government, adopted voluntary taxation and worked out an economic system based on agricultural cooperatives. They had founded forty-four settlements in India, linked by commercial, political and religious ties. In addition, in twenty-three countries, they were keeping the traditional Tibetan culture alive.

Joyce said that in rejecting war, working to restore their human rights by opening nurseries, schools, hospitals and businesses, Tibetans were a pattern for all refugees. Their leader, the Dalai Lama, was one of the strongest human forces for a better world.

12 Out of South Africa

In 1962, before ever Joyce thought of helping non-Europeans, she was driving one of her good friends, Dr Robert Birley, Headmaster of Eton — who was a frequent visitor to Ockenden's Woking houses — back to the school one evening, when he said, almost casually, "I suppose you don't feel Ockenden could look after student refugees from South Africa? I have a feeling, from what I know of that country, that I might become involved with them before long."

Dr Birley, who had led the Education Committee of the British Army of Occupation in Germany at the end of the Second World War, had seen how hardship and deprivation can warp the human personality. In Woking, conversely, he had watched Ockenden's generosity unlock forces of good in displaced European children who, while they had lacked life's necessities, had seemed sad and menacing. Surely such generosity of giving could soothe black South African students who were being mentally and emotionally damaged by apartheid? "What a good idea!" said Joyce. "Yes, I think I can help you."

Months went by, during which Joyce's venture for the Tibetans took Ockenden further towards its multi-national identity. Then she heard again from Dr Birley. He had been appointed Visiting Professor of Education at the University of Witwatersrand in Johannesburg. It was a crucial time in South Africa's history. Only three years earlier, sixty-nine blacks had been killed in the riot at Sharpeville. Three months before Dr Birley's appointment, his friend, Nelson Mandela, the African National Congress leader, had been imprisoned.

By 1963, very few black students were left at the University of Witwatersrand. The 1958 Extension of University Education Act had forbidden their attendance even at universities previously open to them. In any case, only four per cent of blacks attended secondary schools and fewer than one per cent reached the top class. Many black schools had no programme for gifted children. As far as scientific equipment was concerned, four schools in the African townships of Johannesburg, with a total of 3,088 pupils, had between them three microscopes, six balances and thirteen bunsen burners.

Dr Birley found that, though many white students were unhappy about the unfair system, they did not know what to do about it. As contact between black schools and the universities slipped away, he himself kept in touch with black schools. He taught classes in Orlando High School in Soweto, where teachers demonstrated that black students were as intelligent as whites by choosing the most stringent examinations board and the hardest options on syllabuses.

Just as he worked to remove white prejudice against black, so, equally strenuously, Dr Birley tried to destroy black children's prejudice against whites. When they asked him about the Nazis' extermination of the Jews, he replied, "If I promise, when there is a massacre in the Congo, I will not say 'This is what blacks do' but 'This is what some blacks do', will you promise to say about the holocaust not, 'This is what whites do' but 'This is what some whites do'?"

Dr Birley became patron of the South African Committee of Higher Education (SACHED), founded in 1960 with financial assistance from the World University Service. It provided correspondence courses and individual tuition for non–white matriculants, leading to qualifications such as the London University BA and BSc (Econ). Even so, it was far from easy for students to study in the overcrowded townships of Johannesburg and Cape Town. They had no privacy and little time, having to support themselves with full–time jobs.

Dr Birley told Joyce that the National Union of South African students (NUSAS) was raising money for able African students to have a university education in England. "Believe me, they will not get one in South Africa." Could Ockenden look after them, while they studied to reach English university matriculation standard, which was much higher than that of South Africa? They would be twenty-one years of age on arrival, two years older than English students at the same stage.

Joyce's Committee wondered if it would be wise to encourage non-white students to come to England. Inevitably, the students would be granted only exit permits and not allowed to re-enter South Africa. Then they would be cut off from their roots, stranded in England with no guarantee of reaching English university standard.

The committee's objections disappeared when they understood that black South Africans thought of themselves as Africans, rather than as South Africans. They would probably return to other African countries as doctors, economists or teachers. In any case the Home Office agreed that stateless black students could be granted UK citizenship as long as they were not depriving English people of jobs, an eventuality highly unlikely in the sixties. Their potential would be guaranteed both by NUSAS and by Dr Birley. If necessary they could attend classes in English at "The Abbey".

One fact remained. The Ockenden Venture could not use funds donated for East Europeans for South Africans. Another consideration was that since the black students were eighteen, their expenses would be higher than those of the DP children. Joyce began canvassing NUSAS, the Ministry of Education, the United Nations Association, the British Council and various Trusts such as the Gulbenkian Foundation, for money for passports, fares and maintenance. NUSAS would take financial responsibililty when the students reached university, but Ockenden would still be their home.

As their districts deteriorated, the selected black, Cape Coloured and Indian South Africans wrote eagerly to Joyce. In their experience, acceptability had always been determined by community, religion, economic status and race. Now it began to seem as if education might mean individual, social and economic salvation.

The first of the thirteen Africans who came to Ockenden arrived shivering, in tropical clothes. It proved harder than they had expected to adapt to a new climate and a foreign culture and to accept a new relationship with white people. Bruised throughout their lives by discrimination, they were half grateful, half suspicious, at being respected as human beings and made to question their own prejudices.

One boy cracked under the strain. He went out to drown his sorrows in drink. When he came home, he erupted into offensive, anti-white abuse, in danger of creating the racial prejudice he feared even within "The Abbey's" friendly walls. Next morning his hangover was aggravated by remorse. Ivor, a Cape Coloured boy with an Africaans mother and a Chinese father, found it far easier to integrate. He became an elder brother to Joyce's little foster daughter, Veronica, pushing her round and round "The Abbey's" garden in a wheelbarrow.

The South Africans who settled well were those who attended Atlantic College in South Glamorgan. This was the first of the Atlantic sixth form colleges whose aim is to promote understanding in the global village. Kurt Hahn, the co-founder, quoted Sir George Trevelyan's words: "The love of one's country and the love of liberty will not die out but can be kept pure and tamed by love of all mankind." Surrounded by sixth formers of all races and creeds, the South Africans stopped feeling cut off from their own culture. The College offered every academic, physical and artistic opportunity and the students learned to feel needed, helping to operate a cliff, beach and in-shore rescue service.

The Africans bubbled over with personality and self-confidence, contributing to every aspect of college life. Simon Kumalo, whose education in South Africa had been blocked because of his political activity at boarding school, went on to read law at Balliol before becoming a barrister. Seddick Johaddien, who became a student of the University of East Anglia, wrote to Joyce that Norwich might not yet be "very swinging" but certainly would be by the time he left.

His positive experience with Simon and Seddick led the headmaster of Atlantic College to ask Joyce to send him four more South Africans. Simon's elder brother, Livingstone, who had been arrested and imprisoned for belonging to a banned organisation just before he had been due to take up a London University scholarship, was one of those who followed in his brother's footsteps. He later became a master at Atlantic College.

It was necessary for Joyce to move quickly to get boys out of South Africa. They could be arrested at the very last minute, even after they had obtained exit documents. Only one of Ockenden's South Africans reached England without any help, arriving via Leipzig, appearing at Heathrow Airport and asking for asylum, having discovered that, to be educated in Eastern Europe, he would have to become a Marxist.

The arrival of the South Africans caused a flurry of interest among Ockenden's Tibetans, who had never met Africans before. The Tibetans politely asked if they might touch one African boy's hair, which had not been cut for two years. Joyce's belief that if different races could grow up together there would be no racial conflict was confirmed. Africans, Tibetans, Poles and Yugoslavs became a united community with Margaret Dixon at "The Abbey."

They ate, socialised and travelled about together, drawn even closer when one of them, Ali Mohammed Essop, one of the gentlest, most idealistic students ever to come to Ockenden, died during a heart operation. Immediately afterwards, Christmas cards arrived for each of the students signed, "With love from Ali." He had ensured that they were posted the day before his death. His Catholic, Buddhist and Moslem friends and Joyce, Margaret and Dr Christopher Woodard, travelled by minibus to his simple funeral in a London mosque. Shocked out of their usual jovial repartee, the young refugees talked seriously, for the duration of the journey, about one another's situations.

Not long after this, Joyce brought two black Rhodesian girls, Tigwe and Brightness, to "The Abbey." ZAPU (the Zimbabwe African People's Union) had told her that Tigwe and Brightness were trying to exist without any money in London while taking secretarial courses. Having paid for them to come, ZAPU could not support them.

Joyce had no intention of shocking Ockenden's supporters by involving The Venture with ZAPU, an organisation banned in Rhodesia, but she was keen to help Brightness and Tigwe. Both had lost teaching jobs in Rhodesia when black children had boycotted Government schools and both were sure that, as members of ZAPU, they would never obtain new teaching posts. They hoped to gain commercial qualifications which would be of use to Rhodesia in the future, when it would have a black majority government and white workers would leave the country.

Joyce sent Bightness and Tigwe to Abingdon Technical College to finish their secretarial training while living at "The Abbey." Then she persuaded the Ministry of Overseas Development to pay for them at English teacher training colleges and smooth their way back into Rhodesian schools. She gave them and all the Africans new strength and hope, in a world which had inflicted deep wounds upon them simply because of their skin colour and political persuasion.

Simon Kumalo, the South African who became a London barrister, commented that to appreciate the miracle of Joyce's work, one had only to watch her with Margaret at "The Abbey" on Sundays. Surrounded by her multi-national family, she would be sitting with a puzzled look on her face, facing a barrage of questions in languages she had barely heard before. She never reprimanded a member of the community for not speaking English. Nor, as Simon Kumalo put it, did she ever raise her voice according to the well-known English theory, "Shout and ye shall be understood."

13 A School in the Desert

In May 1963, when Joyce's mind was full of the Tibetans, a letter which followed her to Dharamsala directed her thoughts towards a completely different part of the world. It came from Algeria, from Reginald Pollaris, executive secretary to the Council of International Voluntary Agencies, to which the Algerian Government had appealed for help.

France's long occupation of Algeria, followed by Algeria's destructive War of Independence, had caused great hardship. Three million people had died. Thousands had lost their homes. The traditional Arab and Bedouin life-style had broken down. Now, away from the developed coastal strip, there was no employment for the settled inhabitants. Even rich nomads felt insecure, for prolonged periods of drought and bouts of extreme cold had killed whole herds of sheep.

Accompanying voluntary medical teams into isolated villages, Reg Pollaris saw how rapturously the medics were received by chiefs and elders. Seated on the rug-covered floors of rock-walled community huts, they were regaled with pan-fried bread, banana-flavoured soda water, Algerian coffee and mint tea, before being given queues of sick people to examine. Many adults in the villages, as well as children, suffered from skin and bone diseases, blindness and TB, and they had no knowledge of sources of infection. It would never occur to them to brush a fly from the mattery corner of a baby's eye.

Reg decided to centre a "medico-socio" programme on Messaad, the central village or small town of the poorest commune in Algeria, between the last arid slopes of the Sahara mountains.

White Fathers, members of an order of missionaries founded in Algiers in the nineteenth century, moved into Messaad, dug wells for irrigation, started an agricultural commune for twenty families and opened a men's pre-vocational training centre. The Save the Children

Fund set up a nutrition centre with a mother and baby team, and CRS (the Catholic Relief Service) introduced a mobile medical unit.

Messaad's mayor threw his weight and enthusiasm behind the programme, seeing great advantage, in particular, in the Saturday classes in nutrition, hygiene and housekeeping which a CRS nurse was giving to local girls. During the French régime there had been no education for girls in rural districts. Now a new Charter for Women set out to promote a happier future for Algerian women through education. Projects for girls were springing up all over industrially and socially advanced areas. "If only," said the Mayor, "the Messaad classes could be extended!" Reg had no doubt that this would be " a job for Ockenden."

Joyce replied encouragingly to Reg's letter but, before she branched out into another country, she had the summer to survive. First, there was the annual exodus of the DP children to Germany, then she was off to Geneva for more fund-raising. At this time too she lost her secretary. Now that World Refugee Year work was diminishing, Maureen Repassy returned to her own professional career.

Joyce and Margaret were both unwell. Ockenden was paying the price of not being a more structured organisation. Yet that was what made The Venture so flexible, challenging and human. Like any other large family, it was always an adventure of love — and always only just manageable.

Replying to a particularly ambitious suggestion from Reg, that Ockenden should become a high-powered, international development agency (something men, in particular, were always inclined to say), Joyce wrote wearily, "Visions and paperwork have to be brought to reality through endless sacrifice and hard work. Today's problem is how to get to the West Riding in thick fog."

Joyce thought long and hard about the Messaad girls. Reg said they could not cook, except for one or two dishes, and they knew nothing of personal and communal hygiene. Because few of them could sew, they threw torn clothes away. Joyce knew Ockenden must found a school for them.

Though obvious to Joyce, her conclusion struck her Committee like a thunderbolt. "That is the curse of Committees," Joyce wrote to Reg. "One has to have them, then one cannot act in a policy matter of this kind without their consent."

She soon persuaded them that Ockenden, without committing itself to any grandiose schemes, would in future be more generally operational.

Reg, working for the Council of International Voluntary Agencies, knew all about economy. "I do everything myself," he wrote to Joyce. "It is a kind of one-man show. I type my letters and stencils, turn them off, mail and file everything. The lot, what!"

Whether from overwork or in reaction to the Algerian climate, Reg was ill when Joyce (on her way to a conference in Geneva) made a detour to visit Algeria. It was a setback that he could not be there to meet her and show her round. All the same, she set off, undaunted, to the Ministry of Labour and Social Affairs in Algiers, where the Minister himself confirmed that practical education for girls, within the strict framework of Islam, was in keeping with government policy.

Then, in a country where few, if any, women were visible outside industrially developed areas, Joyce set off with an Arab driver, along the rocky desert road to Messaad.

As they entered the village, Joyce noticed how private the single-storey houses were, inside their walled courtyards. How did the women feel, shut up inside? Since births were not registered, the marriage age of sixteen which had been decreed by the Algerian Government in a drive against illiteracy, could not be enforced. Once a girl was fifteen or sixteen, she would never be allowed out again, except perhaps ten times in forty years for family occasions such as weddings. Even these few excursions would be at night, when she would be entirely veiled in a floor-length *haik*, except for the right eye.

A young Messaad wife usually had many confinements in unhygienic conditions. Without knowledge of child care or any recourse to medical help, she would probably lose half her children in their first years. If she was poor, the rest of her life would be a monotonous routine of cooking without the pleasure of shopping; eating, when her husband had finished; cleaning a little, and weaving. Her loom would be thudding away ten or sixteen hours a day, weaving wool or hair she herself had dyed and spun. She would not know how to read, sew or knit and would have no visitors. As if this existence was not drab enough, Islam promised her no joy in the life to come.

Knowing that a school would transform the lives of Messaad girls, Joyce went to work to raise funds for it. Oxfam promised a building grant and Unicef agreed to provide school equipment. Joyce also obtained the services of a talented, thoughtful young architect, David Etherton, who had designed the award-winning revolving sign for New Scotland Yard.

In Messaad, David Etherton found village boys awaiting his arrival. They woke him in the morning, then followed his every move, ready to be on hand if he started doing anything. All wanted to go to France, or anywhere else where they could find work. Here might be a chance to learn a trade!

David designed the school to blend in with traditional desert architecture. Since teachers would always be in short supply, he planned it in the shape of a cross. A central supervision area would overlook four, twenty-foot long rooms radiating from it.

To satisfy Arab modesty, a high wall would have to screen the playground and courtyard from view. He decided to make it ramble, forming curves and alcoves which would create sheltered or sunny places on the outside for men to sit and talk in, after they had done their day's work of shopping and taking the children to school or clinic. Corresponding alcoves and curves on the inside would be pens for poultry.

Since the workmen could not understand the plans, David made a match-stick model. Mohammed ben Ahmed, chief of the village's 500 skilled masons, peering at it through spectacles held together with elastic bands and safety pins, pronounced it a "bonne installation." He was downcast when he knew it was not going to be built out of the hard, white sandstone that was roughly hewn in the mountains and brought down to the village in two unreliable pick-up trucks to be cut into shape. The mud bricks David had in mind would be far cheaper, moulded and dried on site by competing teams of teenage boys.

The ground was too rocky for David to push his carefully-cut wooden pegs into it. He began scratching out the foundations, keeping a wary look-out for scorpions. Then, while one set of workmen dug out the foundations, another constructed a reservoir. All water had to be carried two miles from the nearest river by donkey, at one dinar (8p) a trip.

The scorched concrete roof was supported at intervals by stone columns, rather than on the walls, so that the building could easily be extended in the future. When the roof had been placed on the columns, the masons, who began work at dawn, spent the entire day under it, lying full-length in its shade for their mid-day break, with long strips of white linen pulled over their faces.

Cid Belkasen, the most public spirited man in the village, responsible for everything that worked — the small cinema showing Egyptian romances and warning films about mosquitoes, the electricity generator and the water pump — could hardly believe the masons could be so selfish. Fancy lying down, just when his electrician apprentices were ready to start work! Despite his frustrations, the day came when, armed with straps, cutters and wires, he climbed up the telegraph pole and connected the school's electricity supply.

After the plastering and painting, it was time for glass to be put into the window frames — a feature abhorrent to Arabs, who value privacy so highly. The builders took an age to complete the task, always maintaining that the glass was too thin or the mastic too sticky.

In order to give work to as many people as possible, David employed fifty builders, on a fortnightly basis. They were all involved in the "topping out" celebration. Three sheep were spit-roasted, and two sacks of couscous and twenty kilos of pomegranates consumed.

Just before David's volunteered year was over, Joyce flew to Algeria to see him. He could not stay to see the school complete in every detail, for he had previously contracted to build school refectories further south in the Sahara. Joyce would have to find a replacement for him. Within hours of returning to London, Joyce placed an advertisement in *The Times* for a French-speaking teacher willing to learn Arabic. Within the week, Renée Beach was being met at Algiers airport by David Etherton, having applied, been interviewed and offered the job.

Renée registered at the British Embassy in Algiers, met people in various ministries, said goodbye to David Etherton at the airport and, sooner than she could have believed, headed 500 miles south to her lonely post on the edge of the Sahara.

Bachir, David Etherton's night watchman, became Renée's guide, philospher and friend, as well as her school caretaker. She enjoyed the company and hospitality of the SCF team and the White Fathers, and began to be invited into people's homes so that mothers could discuss their daughters' education.

The village men, who would not have tolerated such behaviour in their wives, did not mind an English woman walking about arranging and administrating. Older women pitied her for being exposed to men's glances. When they had been her age, it was true, they had resented being restricted to their compounds. Now they were grandmothers, they, in their turn, imposed the strict enclosure of young wives.

After her first reactions to a different climate, different food, colours, voices, smells and architecture, Renée adapted well to Messaad life, except that she craved running water. She became resigned to drinking expensive Evian water, rather than waiting twenty minutes for river water to boil, by which time two-thirds of it would have evaporated. River water for washing was delivered in oil drums by the water boy, who pitifully told Renée he was blind. Bachir said, "He, blind? He could see a white hair by moonlight in a bowl of milk!"

Sewing kits, stationery and quantities of scissors from CRS arrived, some of which Renée swopped for SCF tooth paste and tooth brushes. Then a White Father drove up with a hundred olive, acacia and fruit trees. Bachir laboriously dug in two trees, then came running to tell Renée to buy tea and cakes for forty. A commune tree-planting team had appeared in the village and he had asked them in. It took them less than an hour to plant ninety-eight trees.

The Algerian curriculum for an *école ménagere agricole* (a school for girls in rural and domestic science) included moral and civil education, rural legislation, history, geography and science, as well as practical subjects and French and Arabic. Renée knew that she would have radically to adapt the two-year course for Messaad girls, who had never been to school before. Moreover, if she taught the girls too much, they might become discontented with their lives, which were unlikely to change, so far away from developed areas of Algeria. However profoundly fathers doted on their daughters, when the girls became young women, love and paternal pride took second place to the demands of the faith.

While Renée waited for Unicef's educational and husbandry equipment to arrive, she settled in hens and pigeons. Bachir dug a pit from which rabbits could burrow out each day, then return for greenery which he, his children and Renée bought in the market or gathered for them on the dry mountainside. Not realising that Joyce was a vege-

The Ockenden Venture School at Messaad, Southern Algeria

Children in an Ockenden nursery class

tarian, Renée looked forward to telling her how valuable the rabbits would be as a source of protein!

By New Year's Day, the UNICEF equipment had still not arrived. Renée opened the school without it. She expected no more than a dozen pupils, for she had been told that the men would prefer the building to be used as a covered market, rather than as a school. What she had not appreciated was that a father would be able to ask a higher bride price for a daughter who could cook and sew. It would be a particular advantage if she could also speak French. Even after Independence, French methods of administration and the French language continued to be used in Algeria.

Twenty-three girls, aged between ten and fourteen, attended on the first day, their varying needs taxing all Renée's educational ingenuity, especially since her knowledge of Arabic was still elementary. Two could read and write Arabic, none could speak French, four could knit and two could sew.

Anyone who had worked for Joyce for any length of time would have told Renée not to worry. At just the right moment, help would arrive. In fact, two days before the school opened, a Monsieur Gozin had returned from the army, bringing with him his intelligent, serious French wife, who could knit and sew. He was only too pleased to take over the care of his little daughter, escort Madame Gozin to the school each day and leave her in Renée's care as assistant teacher.

Right from the first moment, Messaad's girls became addicted to education. School began to start earlier and finish later, then, to her pupils' delight, Renée introduced school lunches, so that they did not have to leave the premises all day. Unable to see the point of breaks, they had to be forced into the courtyard for recreation.

The girls planted seeds, grew vegetables and, within a few weeks, each had sewn a cushion, a skirt and a blanket of knitted squares. They could form numbers, do simple addition, write the French alphabet and read everyday signs in French and Arabic.

Renée taught them to clean their teeth. Since not one had washed the whole of her body at the same time before, she hired the public bath house once a week for their exclusive use, making towels out of old sheets. The girls thought it amazing to walk through several dark rooms containing mattresses, on which men usually reclined after their baths, then to undress and descend into a dark, steamy cellar. On the sloping floor was a tub of boiling water heated from behind and below, a tub of cold water and several bowls and buckets.

Averting their eyes from the black beatles crawling across the walls, the girls poured water over themselves, washing their hair and bodies and rubbing out their woollies. Afterwards they walked shyly past men queueing to come in.

Renée's girls could be identified as the cleanest, neatest girls around. Medical treatment got underway for their headlice and worms and the bubblings and seethings in their chests caused by active TB. They were vaccinated and careful checks kept of their weight and height.

Eighteen months after the school opened, it was running so smoothly that it seemed appropriate to transfer it to the Algerian system. An Algerian headmistress was appointed and May 13th, 1966 fixed for a handing-over ceremony.

The day before the ceremony, Joyce and a friend of Ockenden, Colonel Ronald Menday, were met at Algiers airport by Renée and David Etherton. As they drove towards Messaad, Joyce was elated by the thought of all that had been achieved since she had first travelled along that rocky road.

She made friends with the school girls, who had laid out their handiwork for her to see, and met people she knew from Renée's letters: the Algerian headmistress, Bachir, Madame Gozin, the White Fathers and the SCF team. Then local dignitaries invited Joyce, Colonel Menday, Renée and David Etherton to a feast in a tent.

Everyone ate standing up, without the help of cutlery, beginning with vegetable and noodle soup then proceeding to mutton, sliced from a spit-roasted sheep. Mutton was followed by chicken, then salad, then sweet couscous — a fresh and dried fruit and grain mixture with lashings of honey. Throughout the mammoth meal, Joyce employed great dexterity and subterfuge to avoid eating meat without hurting anyone's feelings. Since she was a guest of honour, though, she could not avoid being presented with the sheep's eyes on a plate. As she staggered queasily out of the tent afterwards, there was a sudden cry of warning and the thunder of hooves on the desert sand, as camels raced by in her honour, missing her by inches.

The day of the handing-over ceremony dawned hot and clear. At four o'clock in the morning, men built another fire and began turning four more sheep. Then widowed grandmothers arrived to make *chorba*, a kind of soup, couscous and Arab bread. The school girls accompanied them, dark-eyed and beautiful in tinselly festival dresses of purple, scarlet, white or gold.

Fifty guests attended the short ceremony beneath the blossoming trees: local and national govenment officials, representatives of the gendarmarie and the postal service, the educational inspectorate, the White Fathers, the SCF team — everyone who had helped the school on its way. The feast or *meschoui*, which began mid-morning, lasted till late afternoon.

Though the school now belonged to the Algerian Government, Ockenden's interest and good will towards it would continue. At the mayor's request, Renée stayed on in Messaad for two more years. He asked if, in addition to helping in the school, she would conduct a house-to-house census of people's needs. None but she could perform such a task, for men were not allowed into other men's homes.

Months went by before Bachir allowed Renée to meet his wife, who was not at all the savage, desert woman he had described. Renée persuaded him to let his children, Kaddour and Embarka, bring their mother to the school under cover of darkness to chat and drink mint tea with her. She loved Renée to translate the BBC World Service news, though she never could believe it. How could anyone walk on the moon or transplant a human heart?

One night, Bachir's wife was barred from the school by her husband. He sat outside the door, defending a bronchitis-stricken Renée from all visitors with a naked four-foot sword. In her fury, his wife burned a long wound in her arm, knowing that, whenever he saw the scar, he would feel rebuked.

With his new understanding of women's needs, Bachir faithfully kept a promise he made to Renée. Despite constant outside pressure, he resolutely refused to allow Embarka to be married before she turned sixteen.

14 The Saddest Chapter

In some dark places in the world, Joyce's efforts to help destitute children failed utterly. Such was the case in the Lebanon, where evil and conflict had reached such tragic intensity that the difficulties she encountered were insurmountable.

In 1967, an aristocratic Lebanese, Mrs Lamia Moufarrige, invited Joyce and Peter Woodard to Beirut. Having met them at the airport, she whisked them away, in her chauffeur–driven Mercedes, to her "simple" summer retreat in the mountains.

Mrs Moufarrige recognised how unfair and how dangerous it was to allow such disparity as that which existed between rich and poor in the Lebanon. She hoped Joyce would help her found a children's village, to give poverty–stricken children care and education and to act as a model for similar schools and orphanages.

As they sat talking, in a softly–carpeted room, seated on chairs inlaid with mother–of–pearl, Peter's connoisseur's eyes swivelled irresistibly towards Sèvres vases, a Raphael self–portrait and porcelain miniatures of Shakespeare and other English poets. Mrs Moufarrige described a piece of hilly land which she wished to donate for the village, thirty minutes' drive from Beirut, just a short walk from the sea. It was, she said, as attractively sited as one of her own villas, which she used only six weeks a year and which was situated in the middle of olive fields, near St Paul's birthplace, with magnificent views on every side.

After cocktails, other guests arrived, for dinner eaten from Dresden china, using solid silver cutlery, patterned with lilies and carnations. They drank from the finest cut glass that sparkled under ornate chandeliers. Conversation ranged from faith healing (Peter described his brother, Dr Christopher Woodard's, work) to the difficulties for teenagers in this modern world ....

Joyce was impressed that such a wealthy person as Mrs Moufarrige should even notice the suffering of poor children, much less grieve about it. Mrs Moufarrige's husband, whose office was furnished not with desks but with Louis XV tables and chairs, was inclined to think his wife's loving intention a feminine whim. All Mrs Moufarrige's friends seemed incredibly wealthy. Joyce had never seen such an opulent home as that of a princess whom she was taken to visit. Though modern, the room into which she was received was as grand as, and even more beautiful than, the dining room in Buckingham Palace, in which she herself had recently lunched with the Queen.

Joyce wrote to Margaret and Ruth, "It is wonderful that Lamia has asked my advice and help. I hope I will be able to follow this through in the way other things have happened." It was not to be.

Joyce could not differentiate between the needs of poor Lebanese children and those of thousands of Palestinians living in wretched conditions in the Lebanon. Leaving Peter Woodard, who was indisposed, behind, she hired a driver to take her to a Palestinian refugee camp.

They drove through hills covered with square houses, in pastel shades of blue, green and yellow, over desert land, a little cultivated here and there, past Roman remains — a colonnade, a temple and a Roman bath with children swimming in it — to Zous camp near Amman, where the landscape ceased to be picturesque. Hundreds of tents and hovels were crammed together on hilly, desert ground. Seemingly endless queues of undernourished Palestinian children, suffering from eye and stomach infections and sores, led to an SCF medical tent.

Zous camp shocked Joyce less than the Palestinian camp she saw as her car re-entered Beirut. This second camp was unspeakably sordid, sprawling beside a block of luxury flats.

When Joyce talked to the authorities about a small number of Lebanese and Palestinian children growing up together, she encountered a distinct lack of enthusiasm. The Government was opposed to any undertaking which might attract more Palestinians into the Lebanon. Permission for the children's village was revoked.

Depressed and defeated, Joyce returned to England. Not only would Ockenden not be able to help Lebanese children, but a few young Palestinians who could have been educated to live worthwhile, positive lives might grow up to be guerilla fighters. The gap between the Lebanese (particularly the Christian community) and the Palestinians would continue to widen, exacerbated by the intervention of Israel.

Meanwhile the rest of the world failed to help. Millions of dollars of relief were just a palliative. The real problem — of Palestinians, with nowhere else to go, being forced to stay where no one wanted them — was not being addressed.

15   An Evil the World Allowed

As Joyce became internationally known, she spoke out against racial intolerance. When Britain armed Nigeria in its tribal struggle against the Ibos in the part of its territory that became known as Biafra, her voice was one of many calling for an international embargo on both sides.

There had been trouble in Nigeria ever since the British left, for the Constitution which had been bequeathed to it had aggravated racial tension by dividing the country into three parts, each occupied predominantly by one tribe. After a military coup in 1966, the new Federal Government had tried to unite Nigeria under a fresh Constitution. It had failed because the Hausas in the North feared that the ambitious, energetic Ibos in the East would dominate the new civil service.

Waves of massacres of minority Ibos by majority Hausas in the North sent one and a half million Ibo refugees scrambling along roads and railways into the already overcrowded East. There, in retaliation, minority Hausas began to be killed, until they were evacuated for their own safety. General Ojukku, the East's administrator, was a convinced Federalist. He hated racial divisions. His own mother had been burnt to death in sectarian violence. Now, though, he had no choice but to cut off the East from the rest of Nigeria, calling it the independent country of Biafra.

Nigeria's Military Commander, Lieutenant–Colonel Gowon, was determined to keep Nigeria united under one Federal Government, though his intended division of the country into twelve small states would leave the Ibos in small, second class states, cut off from the sea. Afraid that Biafra's secession would lead to moves for independence in other African states, causing more tribal wars, the British Wilson Government supported Lieutenant–Colonel Gowan. Fascist Spain and communist Russia also backed Nigeria. In July 1967, Federal troops entered

Biafra.

The small, poorly-equipped, blockaded Biafran army, with just a trickle of support from other West African countries, was maintained by the Biafran people. Cobblers made army boots from canvas, tailors sewed uniforms from curtaining, farmers contributed produce and bushmen provided blunderbusses and axes. Taxis, bicycles and mammy-wagons made up the short-fall in army trucks. Even the poorest villages collected money.

The Biafran army not only resisted attack. It also dared to invade the West, to liberate some small tribes. With massive shipments of arms from Britain and Russia, the Federal Army exacted terrible revenge. As Biafran towns fell, more people were killed in ten weeks than in the first three years of the Vietnam war.

Biafran economic life slumped. Thriving urban groups turned into bands of squatters living on army hand-outs. The country became cut off from imported protein — meat from northern Nigeria; dried stockfish from Scandinavia. Biafra lost its food-rich southern and northern edges, yet from them had to absorb five million refugees. During the next eighteen months, one million Biafrans starved to death. What had been the fastest developing part of Nigeria had become the most desolate.

In 1968, the Year of International Rights, television news shocked the world with pictures of starving Biafran children — serving the propaganda interests of both sides in the conflict. The Federation used the pictures to convince the divided Wilson Cabinet that it should supply more arms, to bring the war to a quick, humane end. The Biafrans pointed to the pictures as proof of genocide. Kwashiokor, the malnutrition-related illness, in which skin becomes pale, hair reddens, joints swell and flesh becomes bloated, became officially termed the "Harold Wilson disease" on Biafran death certificates.

Joyce, Margaret Dixon, Ruth Hicks, Sir Robert Birley and Dr

Christopher Woodard, agonising over Britain's responsibility, wrote to *The Times*, asking how British people could reconcile their sympathy with the sufferings of the Czechs and the Vietnamese with their shamefaced acquiescence in the agony of Commonwealth children in Biafra. In fact, many British people were feeling impotent rage at the news of unsuccessful cease-fires; the shooting down of a Red Cross plane; obstacles put by both sides in the way of land and sea corridors; the bombing of civilians and hospitals and the suggestion that food aid would prolong the war.

When it was suggested, not by Joyce but during a television programme on which she appeared, that 10,000 starving Biafran children and babies should be air-lifted to England for a year, she became the focus of hope. Letters poured in to her from people desperate to help: from Wales, "We live on a farm. We have plenty of room for an extra two"; from Berkshire, "We would like to know that we have saved just one"; from the Cotswolds, "The air is fresh and healthy here. We have a large garden they can use when they are better. They would grow well and strong"; from London, "I am sixty-one. If I can help by caring for a Biafran baby it will be surrounded by love. It is the only thing I can do."

This time, Joyce felt, the dynamic of compassion was wrongly focussed. Her mind reeled at the thought of starving African infants farmed out all over the British Isles, with loving people whose generous response would probably not equip them to communicate with non-English speaking children or to cope with emotional, medical and dietary problems. She made sure each letter received a grateful, comforting reply, saying that, if any Biafran children did arrive, Ockenden would care for them in groups. All the same, it would be infinitely preferable for the Biafrans to remain in an environment like their own.

"If only people's concern could be harnessed to positive effect!" Joyce thought. If public opinion could be seen to be powerful enough to

Evacuated Biafran children outside the temporary hospital tent in Libreville, Gabon

Richard Todd, the actor, loyal supporter of Ockenden, seen here on his *This is Your Life* Programme in 1960 with Joyce and other friends and colleagues

end the Biafran war, people might stop ignoring the suffering that goes on all the time somewhere in the world, except when consciences are sharply pricked and thoughts focussed on particular crises by television.

Joyce and her friends mounted a two-pronged attack on the suffering and on the war. In July 1968, Dr Woodard flew to Biafra to find out how Ockenden could help children. At home, Joyce campaigned to halt the despatch of arms to Nigeria.

Flying from Biafra to Rome, Dr Woodard arranged for The Ockenden Venture to co-operate with Vatican-based Caritas. Caritas had obtained permission from the Biafran authorities for 3,000 children to be flown by the Red Cross to the Ivory Coast, the Portugese colony of Aso Tome and the island of Gabon, a former French colony. It was in Gabon, which had offered to take 20,000 children, on condition that it was given international assistance, that Ockenden arranged to work.

In September 1968, when the war was fourteen months old, 100,000 people dead and thousands starving, thousands of desperately ill children and babies were carried off planes at Libreville, the capital of Gabon. Some people said that such weak children should not be moved. In fact, many died. Other critics had warned that under cover of the air lifts Biafra might rearm. What was certain was that thousands of children were saved from violence and starvation.

Before the children arrived, Father Pinus of the local Sainte Marie Mission set up feeding and medical centres in Gabon. Dr Woodard collected a team of British and Biafran doctors and nurses to fly out from London but, at the last moment, the Gabonese Government refused to accept the team. It believed in the goodwill of the Ockenden Venture but would not trust anyone from a country which was still arming Nigeria. Only one member of the team, Claire Glorieux, whom Joyce had met in a social and refugee medical centre in Jordan, was allowed to enter Gabon, because she was Belgian.

Claire, a paediatric social worker and a member of the International

Catholic Auxiliaries, helped Father Pinus prepare three large sheds, one with fifty-seven beds, one with eighty-one and one with thirty-six mattresses on the floor. Her staff would consist of forty French, Australian and Irish teachers and nurses.

Three hundred weak, feverish children, aged between one and twelve years, arrived in Gabon, then thirty or so more children every day until, by April 1969, numbers had reached 700. In December 1968, Claire was already writing to Joyce to say that though at first two children had died every day, 250 were now going to school. "So clever and full of jokes — hilarious!" An eight-room school was built and a dispensary with fifty beds. By Christmas children's village would have been constructed.

"The spirit between all the personnel is excellent," Claire wrote. "We are happy to work in poverty and to help as much as possible. Our day's work is twelve to fourteen hours non-stop, but when we are a complete team it will be all right.

"It is very hot but, in the evening, a wind blows off the sea. Every morning I do the dispensary on the terrace. I have one child sitting on my chair with me and one on each side with their heads on my knees, and so I must work. They do so much need affection."

At mid-day on Christmas Eve, a plane landed from Paris bringing toys which Claire's helpers gift-wrapped all afternoon. They held a feast in the evening, followed by Biafran songs and dances and a nativity play in French. A boy called Simon stepped forward and made an impromptu speech of thanks to Father Pinus, who was too overcome with emotion to reply.

Through *The Times Educational Supplement*, Joyce had asked every British person to say a prayer at midnight on Christmas Eve for the children left in Biafra. In Haslemere, twelve Biafran children and their British-born mothers were praying for peace. They said Biafrans would never have wanted secession, if only they could have felt secure inside the Federation of Nigeria.

The Biafran children and their mothers joined Polish, Latvian and Lituanian children, Czech families and a Rhodesian family in "Keffolds" for a noisy, joyful Christmas Day. Meanwhile, in Libreville, the Biafran children attended an Ibo service in the cathedral, after which the Apostolic Delegate of Equatorial Africa distributed the toys.

In May, Group–Captain Leonard Cheshire organised a relief ship to sail from Liverpool to West Africa by way of Libreville. Ockenden supporters collected £2,000 worth of school equipment, knitted blankets, clothes, toys, soap, fourteen sacks of rice, tins of pilchards (Claire said the children ate 100 tins of pilchards every two days) and tins of corn beef, baked beans and grapefruit segments. Joyce addressed one tea chest to Claire, packing it with toiletries and tissues, jam, mushroom soup, sweets and washing powder.

As Eric Jones drove the Ockenden lorry onto the docks at Liverpool, mountains of crates and boxes from all over Britain were being crammed into the hold of the relief ship. The Merseyside dockers who were doing the loading were on strike where other ships were concerned. They were donating their day's wages to the relief fund. Ignoring demarcation rules they helped drivers haul boxes from vans and lorries, upset to learn that a slightly-built nun had unloaded seven heavy crates before anybody saw her. They were shaken by the speed with which Liverpool students unloaded chest after chest from their old pantechnicon, which had lurched onto the docks under the weight of its load.

Claire wrote to Joyce to describe the arrival and opening of the boxes in Gabon; the pride of older boys strutting about in new shirts and shorts; the delight of Biafran teachers at finding so many useful articles. She had been touched to find her own personal tea chest from Joyce and "ecstatic" over the mushroom soup. Father Pinus, who could not speak English, asked her to convey his deep gratitude to British people.

Meanwhile, ironically, the British Government continued sending shells, armoured cars and ammunition to Nigeria. *The Times* leader of June 28th 1969 commented:

> Only the capacity of the human mind to steel itself against large figures and abstract terms makes it possible for this policy to be pursued. Men who would not willingly harm a single infant, find it tolerable to support a policy of starvation by the million.

Joyce, on the executive of the Committee for Action on Nigeria and Biafra, concentrated on galvanising the indignation of young people, who would soon be voting in their first General Election. Surely, they had the power to influence events! At a symposium she hosted at "Quartermaine," representatives of the Young Conservatives, Young Liberals and Young Socialists signed a public request for the Government to bring about an international embargo on Nigeria and Biafra and unilaterally to stop arming Nigeria.

The Archbishop of Canterbury gave the document his blessing. Cardinal Heenan, at a mass for Biafrans in Westminster Cathedral, said, "It is well known that this country and Soviet Russia are supplying many of the instruments for the destruction of your homes and families. You know most of our people are ashamed to be in any way responsible for your suffering."

No arms embargo came about. In January 1970, in the face of tremendous fire power, the Biafran troops, many of whom had not eaten for weeks, surrendered. Their leader, General Ojukwu, flew to exile in the Ivory Coast.

Though reunification was not followed by genocide, the fear of which had kept Biafrans fighting for so long, the war left a legacy of bitterness. Claire's Biafran doctors and nurses received letters telling of unpaid Ibo workers, suppressed Ibo industry and murdered Ibo intellectuals. Four hundred Ibo children were dying of starvation every day.

Claire and Father Pinus were alarmed when, for reasons of their own, Germany and America supported the immediate repatriation of Ibo children. Only two out of 850 parents asked for their children to return straight away. In any case, sixty Ockenden children had no parents. If they were sent back to Nigeria at once, they would languish in refugee camps far worse than the children's village in Gabon.

Joyce flew to Geneva to urge governments not to allow the children to be used as political pawns. Agreeing with her, the United Nations High Commissioner for Refugees, Prince Sadruddin Aga Khan, insisted no children should return home until safe reintroduction policies had been worked out.

It was, therefore, not until November that, gradually and properly, repatriation began. Families were traced with the help of churches, missions and SCF. When the process was almost complete, the Lagos Government invited representatives of those who had cared for the children, including Claire and Father Pinus, to visit Nigeria.

Although they were received coldly in Lagos, Claire and Father Pinus were overwhelmed by parents' gratitude in what was now called East Central State. Their arms were filled with more bananas than they could carry. Children who had returned to families were lively, healthy and happy, even when money was scarce. They were attending schools which, though pillaged during the war, were clean and orderly.

Children who had lost their families were not so content. One boy, who had left Nigeria as a baby, was particularly lonely. His parents had rejected him because they had already taken in a child they believed to be theirs.

On the whole, Claire and Father Pinus were satisfied with what they found. Four per cent of children, it was true, still languished in transit centres, so thin and bored as to be hardly recognisable as the vigorous children who had left Gabon. Some of them would have to go to orphanages but most would be adopted by parents whose own children had died.

Biafrans, trapped in England by the war, were out of their minds with worry, not having heard from their families for four years. The Ockenden Venture invited them to write to Rev. Igwe, in Woking. He sent a missing persons' list to church councils in Nigeria. He had been reunited with his own four children at Ockenden, and also with his wife, a teacher, who had been a nurse in the Biafran front line.

Bad news frequently had to be broken, but there were many happy endings. A doctor at least knew that his wife and childen were safe when he received a letter showing the strain they had been under. "I have long hungered to see you. Just imagine, six weeks is now four years. The children are much worried too. Please wangle your way home. Come back and enlighten my way once more."

When families were found, the Home Office soon processed their papers, though Lagos bureaucracy seemed intent on slowing things down. One man was shot at as he queued for emigration papers.

While Nigeria underwent its long restorative process, Cynthia Gunn, an Australian Ockenden volunteer, continued looking after six English-speaking Nigerian children in Woking. Having been reticent and insecure, they had soon been drawn into the activities and homes of fellow pupils at Greenfield School, and into the Scouts, Girl Guides and Girls' Brigade. If they were still sometimes serious, it was not because they were remembering the horrors they had seen. They were missing Nigeria's bush and pine forests.

To Joyce the six symbolised thousands of children whose families, education and potential had been savaged by an evil the world had tolerated. She hoped that now a new spirit of brotherhood, without exploitation or prejudice, would encourage a rebirth of happiness in Nigeria.

1969. Three children from two trouble-torn countries with friends from Greenfield School. Biafran twins, Nmeke and Gmeka Dike, and, on their left, David Marx from Czechoslovakia. Courtesy T and J Colour Photography, Worplesdon

Ruth Hicks and Margaret Dixon in the 1970s

16 Project Vietnam

In February 1971, Susan Spenser, who had once worked for Ockenden in India, invited Joyce to visit war-torn South Vietnam, to see how Ockenden could help a few of the hundreds of thousands of war orphans whose numbers were overwhelming even the world's largest agencies.

Vietnam had suffered so many years of terrible conflict that it was hard to imagine the tranquil, fertile, sub-tropical country it had once been. Before the ravages of modern warfare, jagged timbered mountains had fallen through rich green jungle to flat, fertile rice-growing areas around the Red River Delta in the North and the Kong Delta in the South, while along the long, craggy coastline, sampans and fishing junks were etched on a sparkling sea.

In the seventeenth century, French Jesuit missionaries to Vietnam had remarked on the loving, easy disposition of the Vietnamese. Their religion, a profound synthesis of Buddhism, Confucianism and Taoism, was a source of unity, each village having a central pagoda for meetings, celebrations and prayer. The extended family provided additional security.

Since that time, unity and the feeling of security had been assaulted by successive waves of warfare and conquest. French colonial rule gave way to Japanese, then, after the Japanese surrender, the country — now called the Democratic Republic of Vietnam — was briefly controlled by a coalition of revolutionary communists (the Vietminh) under Ho Chi Minh. Then the French recaptured the part of Vietnam called Cochin China.

With arms supplied by communist Russia and China, the Vietminh fought the French, who were supported by America. Ordinary Vietnamese people were caught up in the crossfire for seven years, until in 1954, the French lost the battle of Dien Bien Phu. By the Geneva Accords, until elections could decide South Vietnam's future, Vietnam was divided along the 17th Parallel. The communist North continued to be supported by China and a million Catholic refugees fled to the South, which was ruled by the Catholic general, Ngo Dinh Diem.

Supported by President Eisenhower, who feared that South East Asia's non-communist régimes would fall like a row of dominoes if South Vietnam voted for communism, Diem refused to hold elections. North and South became separate, hostile countries, and the Vietnamese war began.

By 1966 Central Vietnam was harbouring one million refugees from both North and South. Collectivization in the North had mercilessly eliminated landlords and rich peasants. In the South, Diem had used police to restore rich landlords, consolidating his family's power, spreading Catholicism by force and cracking down on Buddhism.

When the South Vietnamese saw 540,000 American soldiers supporting Diem's hated régime, corrupting women and children with dollars, humiliating the elderly by dislocating families, abandoning civilised behaviour as they fought a hopeless war in a jungle, thousands joined the Vietcong.

To flush out Vietcong guerrillas, the Americans bombed both North and South, razed villages, burned crops, defoliated and bull-dozed thousands of acres of woodland. In Operation Cedar Falls in 1967, helicopters warned peasants to leave 8,000 forest villages, causing men, women, children, babies, ducks, chickens, dogs and buffaloes to surge down highways, priests and village chiefs trying to lead them to safe areas, before these too were demolished.

Operation Junction City in May 1967 took 3,000 Vietcong lives, but in 1968 the Tet offensive turned the tide. Now that 57,000 Americans had died, US troops started to be withdrawn. Yet America still supplied money, weapons and air support to South Vietnam. In 1970, North Vietnam, including the cities of Hanoi and Haiphong, was bombed, while North Vietnam attacked the South.

Thirty years' onslaught had produced ten million victims: millions burnt and poisoned by dioxin and agent orange; a million disabled children; innumerable neglected, starving, disease-ridden orphans.

****

It was nine o'clock at night with a hot breeze blowing, when, in February 1971, four years before the North Vietnamese took Saigon, Joyce and Dr Christopher Woodard alighted with other civilian passengers at Saigon Airport. Armed guards manned barriers, soldiers patrolled in jungle green and brown and American trucks and transport planes were lined up behind barbed wire.

Joyce and Dr Woodard saw Susan Spenser waving to them, thinner and browner than when she had returned from working for Ockenden with Tibetans. She now worked for PVO (Project Vietnam Orphans), an English Christian adoption agency, in Hoi duc Anh, a Saigon orphanage.

In a ramshackle Land Rover passed on by a British medical team, Susan drove Joyce and Dr Woodard along Cong-Ly Street into the brilliantly-lit centre of Saigon. Iron grilles protected restaurants, cafés and bars which were as thronged with customers as the pavements were full of mollusc-hatted people buying and selling at stalls or crouching, hands cupped around steaming bowls, beside charcoal stoves. From the heart of the teaming city, Joyce, Susan and Dr Woodard walked into the polite atmosphere of a diplomatic party in the British consular house where Joyce was to stay. The guests were relieved to hear why Joyce had come, for they knew that there were 300,000 orphans in Saigon, of whom a mere 20,000 were in orphanages.

To demonstrate what medical facilities were available for mutilated and handicapped Saigon children, Sue took Joyce and Dr Woodard to the orthopaedic section of a Government-sponsored hospital. The medical team fitting artificial limbs were British, for Vietnam had only

400 civilian doctors for its seventeen million population. All Saigon hospitals were understaffed. In addition, as US troops withdrew, US Army medical units, which had previously been open to Vietnamese, closed down.

Celia Barclay, wife of one of the hospital doctors, told Joyce and Dr Woodard that she foresaw the sea of orphans turning into an army of pathologically disturbed teenagers, unless something was done to stimulate them and give them individual care and love. Vietnam had no history of child welfare work. In the past, the system of the extended family had made it unnecessary. For the well-being of the rest of the world, as well as for Vietnam, help must come from outside.

Celia had opened a children's day care centre to keep children with one parent out of orphanages by freeing the parent to work. So many husbands had been killed or maimed that many new mothers with dependant children slipped out of maternity hospitals in the night, abandoning their new-born babies. Many illegitimate sons and daughters of American servicemen were also disowned and queues of women formed at the gates of the orphanages every morning, trying to give away children they could not feed. More women "lost" their children in the milling streets.

Celia introduced Joyce to Vietnamese women whom she was training to tour the poorest areas of the city in a mobile play centre, giving children living at home one or two hours' mental stimulation every day. She took her to visit some Buddhist monks who were making toys and learning aids for the play centre in a factory beside their pagoda. Joyce promised that Ockenden would support Celia's projects financially and send trained nursery workers from England.

Most of Joyce's few days in Saigon were spent exploring options for The Ockenden Venture, though she managed incidentally to enjoy a few Vietnamese delicacies such as fried prawns in batter, baked in sugar cane. The British Ambassador and his wife were extremely helpful, as was Mr Phieu, the Vietnamese minister of social affairs, who said The Ockenden Venture would be registered as a South Vietnamese charity. He agreed, in principle, to a few Vietnamese having nursery training in England, though, from past experience, he knew such courses were despised by academic Vietnamese girls.

Hoi duc Anh orphanage, where Sue Spenser worked, was run by the Cao–Dao ladies, members of a sect whose beliefs, as defined by Hugo Gurdon in the *Daily Telegraph* in November 1991, were "a soup of Buddhism, Taoism and Confucianism, seasoned with Christianity, Islam and a pinch of local beliefs." They supported the South Vietnamese Government, continuing to defy communism even after the end of the war.

Hoi duc Anh was in the centre of the city. To reach it, Sue drove Joyce and Christopher past a turreted Buddhist pagoda, across a filthy stream with rice growing on its banks, into a narrow lane of flat–roofed, white–washed houses, shacks and a market with a rubbish dump, behind which was the orphanage. In a dirty courtyard, inside a wall fortified with barbed wire, Joyce and Dr Woodard met a tumble of barefoot urchins, whose sore–covered skins were splashed with red mercurichrome. The children hugged the visitors' legs, fingering Joyce's dress and touching her handbag, staring up in astonishment at Dr Woodard, who seemed so tall. Other children were being sluiced under a tap, near filthy toilet holes in which black rats, nine to ten inches long, were snuffling. In a dark kitchen, without electricity or tap, a Vietnamese woman was boiling rice in black pots over a charcoal fire. From under the kitchen table came a great clucking of chickens in a cage.

In a second building, sixty toddlers were confined to cots with no one to play with them. Sue told Joyce that, when sometimes they were put altogether into a twenty–foot pen on the tiled floor, they would press their faces to the bars in the hope of attracting a glance from somebody.

In this unlikely setting, Tony Williams, a PVO worker, had established a typewriting and accountancy course for older children, every single one of whom he would have transported to England if he could. Elizabeth, his wife, had started a primary class, whose children folded their arms and bowed when Joyce and Dr Woodard entered. In another room, Sue had begun a playgroup.

In Room 4, forty handicapped children lay on plank beds or fell off onto the floor, wet with urine and covered in excreta. Those who were not orphans had been rejected by their parents because of some deformity, the slightest handicap, even a hare lip, being considered a sign of evil-doing in a previous life. All had sores, inflammation of the ears and flies buzzing round eyes and mouths. The mentally retarded lay gazing at the ceiling.

Since Hoi duc Anh babies had to feed themselves from bottles propped on pillows, it was hardly surprising that all of them were undernourished. Older ones, who scooped up cereal with their hands from bowls on the floor, shared their food with rats.

Joyce and PVO agreed that Ockenden would take over the sponsorship of Hoi duc Anh, leaving PVO to concentrate on its adoption policies and upon other orphanages. Ba Kuen, the fat, kindly Principal, looked forward to the arrival of Ockenden nursery staff from England, who would train nursery nurses and at the same time improve the orphanages' facilities. Joyce returned home determined to find a sponsor for every child.

For some time, British television viewers had been distressed to witness the suffering of the Vietnamese. Their compassion found an outlet when an appeal by Ingrid Bergman focussed minds on the particular orphans Joyce had visited in Hoi duc Anh.

Families, individuals, organisations and schools volunteered to sponsor the orphans, five hundred children in one primary school deciding to give a penny a week each, in addition to holding fund-raising events. The staff of Crewkerne Hospital became a thirteen-year-old Vietnamese boy's "family."

A sponsorship was promised not only for every child in Hoi duc Anh but also for each of the children in Ky Quano, another orphanage. Enough money was sent to support twelve Ockenden British and Vietnamese staff, to train more Vietnamese women and to improve the orphanage.

Renée Beach, who, when she was eight, had briefly lived in Saigon, where her father had been Consul, had returned from working in Ockenden's school in Algeria. Trained as a physiotherapist, she was exactly the right person to be Ockenden's Vietnam administrator. She rented a Saigon house — No. 23, Ky Dong Street — from which she organised work in the orphanages, initiated home visits, play groups and clinics, started an immunisation scheme and began tracing families and processing birth certificates.

No. 23, Ky Dong Street became a day care centre for sixteen handicapped children, who were taken there every morning from Hoi duc Anh and Ky Quano. The van that brought them returned to the orphanages with huge containers of rice, meat bone and vegetable stew and, since fresh milk was unobtainable, sweetened condensed milk diluted with water. Continuity was maintained over four years until 1975. Renée handed over to Barbara O'Hara, a nurse and midwife, and Barbara to Margaret Dolan, a physiotherapist.

With the handicapped children's daily ration of love and exercise, despite the primitive conditions to which they returned each night, their mobility improved rapidly. Renée was sure they would be able to get rid of their old-fashioned, wooden crutches and parts of their heavy calipers if they could have treatment in England. If the Saigon authorities saw the children becoming independent, they might be encouraged to improve their own facilities.

Renée obtained Vietnamese Government approval for five child polio victims, Lan, Minh, Thuy, Kim Chi and Ngoc, to fly to England, on condition that they learned no English and returned to Saigon within a year. Special sponsors were found and the Far East Travel Company paid the girls' fares.

On 9th February 1973, the five little girls were carried off an aircraft at Heathrow. Waiting with the Press to receive them were Joyce, whom they later adopted as their *Ba Noë* or grandmother; the Rt. Hon. David Ennals, then chairman of Ockenden; Diane Worsley, a young Australian psychiatric nurse, who was to give them loving care and supervise their programme throughout their time in England; and Silvia Johnson, a trained residential worker. They were taken to "Keffolds," given warm baths and food and settled into an airy bedroom in their own wing, overlooking the downs and the garden.

The community of refugees in "Keffolds," and some visiting Tibetan lamas, made a great fuss of the children. Otherwise they were kept in a Vietnamese atmosphere in their own part of the house. Madeleine, a young, pretty Vietnamese teacher who had come to England with them, helped to care for them and taught them their first ever lessons. Diane and Sylvia struggled to learn a few words of the difficult Vietnamese language in which one word has many meanings, depending upon how it is pronounced.

To ease the children's return to Vietnam, they were insulated from treats such as sweets and chocolates, which they might miss later. Since they were Catholics, they were taken to Haslemere's Catholic church each Sunday, where they enjoyed taking part in the familiar ritual of the mass.

Nuns at Holy Cross Hospital in Haslemere offered physiotherapy facilities free of charge. Mr McLeod Baikie, consultant orthopaedic surgeon at Great Ormond Street Hospital, also waived his fees, finding the Vietnamese children's strain of poliomyelitis easier to treat than

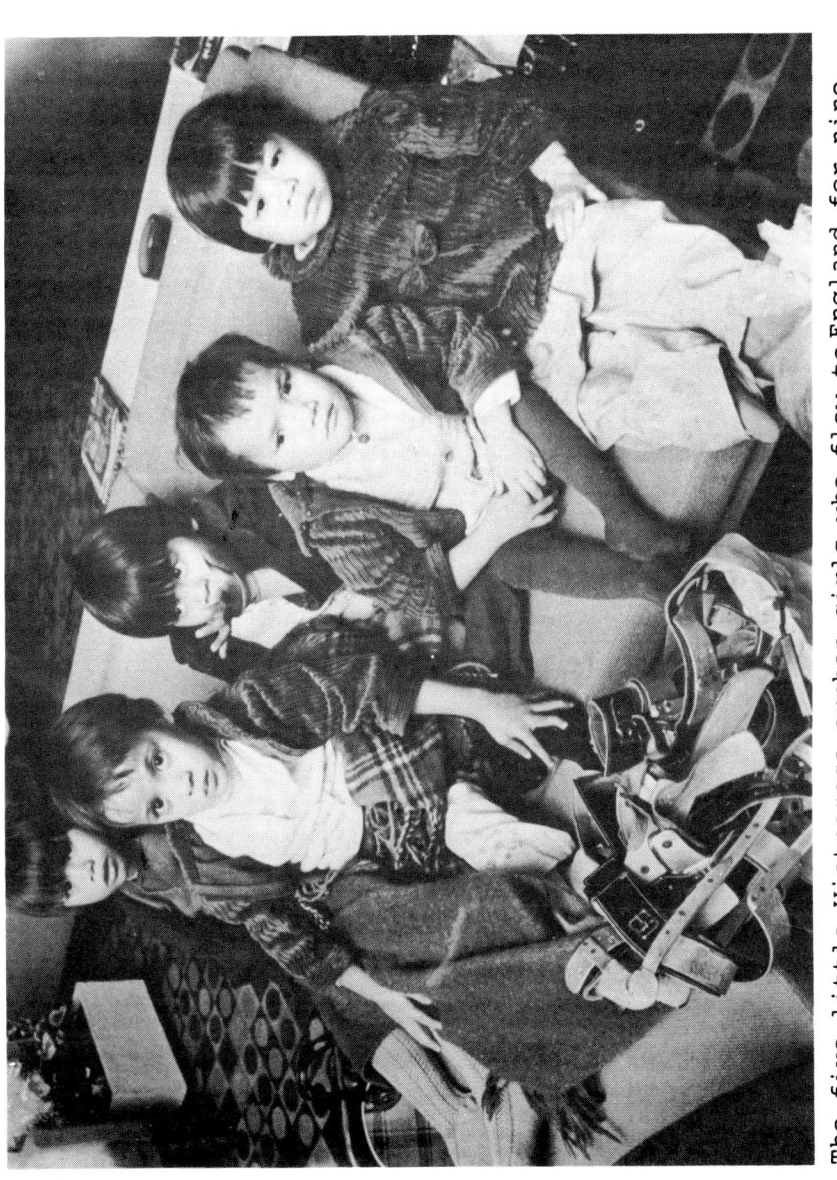

The five little Vietnamese orphan girls who flew to England for nine months' orthopaedic treatment in February 1973. Courtesy Daily Mail

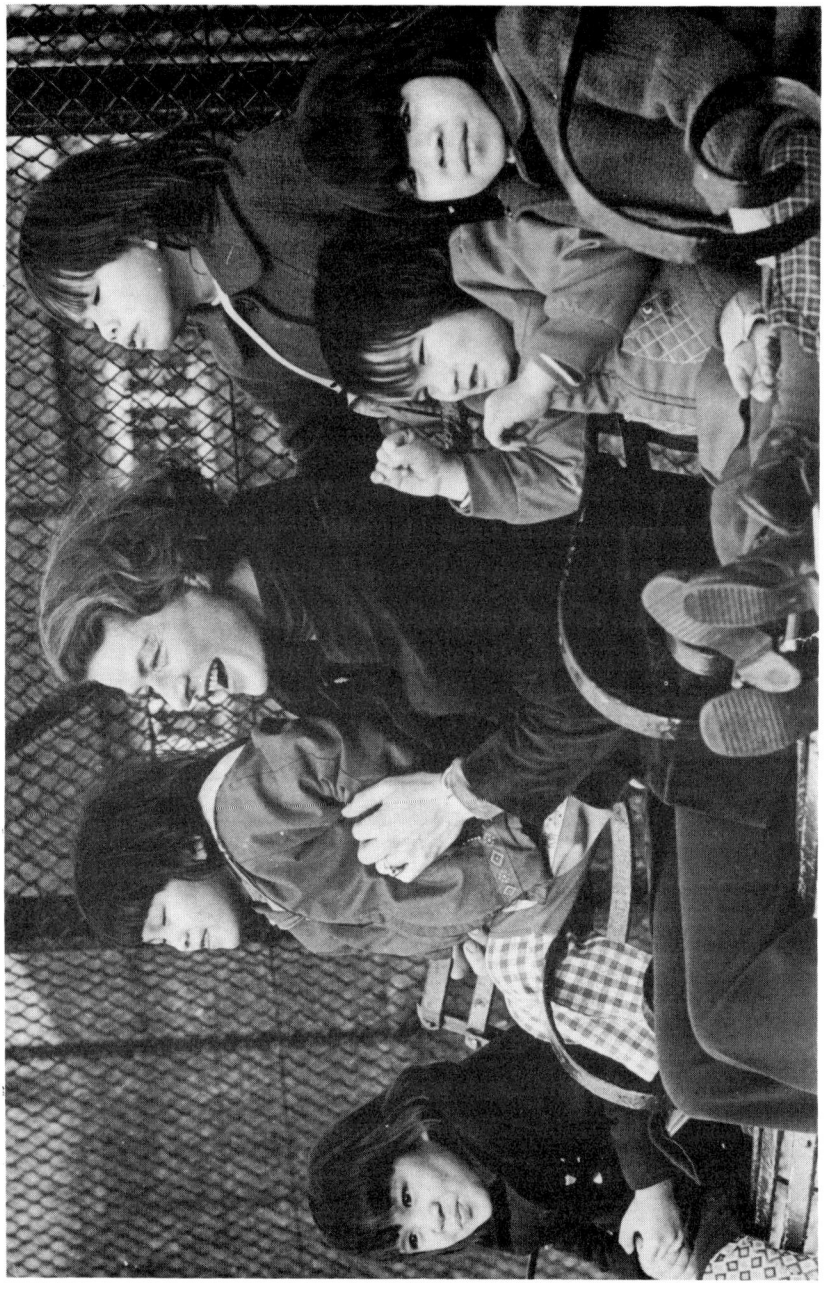

The actress Ingrid Bergman with the "famous five" at London Zoo.

that found in the West. Some of the girls' leg muscles were wasted, but other muscles grew strong with exercise and with sessions in Haslemere's heated pool, paid for by Haslemere Scouts.

Before everyone's eyes, the children began to change, stand without crutches and shed bits of caliper. Their sponsors, who came regularly to see them, were captivated by their big smiles, effervescent temperament and cheerful self-confidence.

Ingrid Bergman loved them. Just before they were due to return to Vietnam, she took them to London Zoo and bought them toys from the shop. She rocked with laughter when they burst into song in the restaurant, singing a Vietnamese version of *Frère Jaques* (which is all about a butterfly) in thin, high Vietnamese voices, *One Man and His Dog*, which Diane and Silvia had taught them, and *Yellow Submarine*, which they did not understand but had picked up from the radio.

There was no way Joyce could contemplate sending the children back to their rat-ridden orphanage, after having let them experience a Western life-style, though she could not avoid sending them back to Vietnam. As the time for their return drew near, they panicked at the thought of it. Joyce appealed to everyone on The Ockenden Venture mailing list to send fifty pence towards a small, residential handicapped centre in Saigon. Then, as the money came in, she prayed for a physiotherapist. Margaret Dolan immediately rang up, volunteering to go to Vietnam. She went to stay at "Keffolds", to get to know the children and to try out physiotherapy techniques for a Third World country.

In November 1973, nine months after the children had been carried into Heathrow, they walked out to their plane hand-in-hand, bravely singing *One Man and his Dog*, to the delight of cameramen. None had crutches, and only three wore complete, lighter versions of calipers. The other two had just one caliper each.

Madeleine, the Vietnamese teacher, wept to see them go, for she was not returning to Vietnam.

****

While Lan, Thuy, Kim Chi, Ngoc and Minh were living peacefully in Haslemere, the war crept closer to Saigon. When Joyce again visited the city, there was a sentry outside the Ockenden house, whose warning gunfire disturbed the curfew hours.

Ba Kuen welcomed Joyce with flowers, so grateful that the children in Hoi duc Anh were now having individual attention and the babies being properly fed. Rats still scampered about, but, Joyce was assured, that was normal in Saigon. The dark, primitive kitchen had been rebuilt.

Only the orphanage's horrific reception procedures remained unchanged. When screaming orphans were tugged to the gate, an angry-looking woman, one eye glaring fiercely, the other, made of glass, dangling out of its socket, grabbed children by their wrists and dragged them inside, locking the gate behind them.

Four-year-old Duong arrived, clinging to the policeman who had found him. When the policeman left, the little boy hurled himself at the gate screaming, while other children gathered round laughing. Joyce had to go out for a few hours. When she returned, Duong was still screaming, by now chained to his bed.

With Diep, a Vietnamese member of staff, translating, Joyce coaxed Duong into telling her he was not an orphan. He had a mother, father and three brothers and could identify his house, if only someone would take him to a bridge he named.

Joyce asked for the key to his padlock and set him free. Then she and Diep took him to the bridge by taxi. Once there, he identified every shack among thousands in the alleyways as his. Finally, as it grew dark, he sank onto the ground in a defeated heap.

Joyce was beginning to despair too, when an older boy slid out of the shadows, said he recognised Duong, did not know where he lived but could find his brothers. Next morning, after Duong's mother had collected him from Ky Dong Street, Joyce wondered how many hundreds of other boys had been lost in the milling streets and were trapped in orphanages because nobody had time to identify them.

Joyce chose two more institutions for Ockenden to support. The first was An Loc refugee camp on the other side of the wide River Mekong, where 2,000 lean, black–haired, dark–skinned mountain people — the Montagnards — were living, the men dressed in loin cloths or shorts, the women wearing ground–length skirts. In their former, jungle conditions, now destroyed by bombing, they had had no problems about survival. Here, in alien, flat countryside, two miles from running water, with no possessions apart from the coconut mats on which they slept and a few pots and pans, they were suffering from malnutrition and disease. Joyce promised to send help to the one doctor and three nurses who were running a clinic for the whole camp.

Funds, rather than personnel, were needed by a Vietnamese priest, Father Hoan, who, during the 1972 Tet offensive in which 40,000 died, had led a column of children out of Quang Tre Province near the 17th Parallel, on a two–month trek to Saigon. His Street Boys' Project, a children's community, had help from local doctors and dentists but no staff, for older boys looked after younger ones. When Joyce called they were finishing tea, washing up and neatly stacking plastic plates and cups. Father Hoan had taught them to grow vegetables, ground nuts, sweet potatoes and pampas grass, and to keep pigs and chickens. They also had what looked like Jersey cows, telling Joyce, to her indignation, that they killed one cow a month for protein as milking was too complicated. "No wonder there is no fresh milk in Saigon!" she wrote to Margaret and Ruth.

Father Hoan's achievements made Joyce keener than ever for The Ockenden Venture to educate men and women of imagination and initiative to rehabilitate their own people. Whereas no amount of foreign aid on its own could do any good, moderate funding of energetic, practically-trained individuals could produce long-term improvements. She promised to send funds to Father Hoan.

Joyce visited Saigon again, for the last time as it turned out, in the autumn of 1974. She was anticipating building on Ockenden's work in Vietnam, for a recent appeal by Ingrid Bergman had raised £4,000.

The city seemed positively dangerous. On the day before National Day, October 31st, demonstrators blocked the streets, pickets of soldiers made travel impossible and the market was surrounded by armoured cars. Crowds accumulated. Smoke bombs were thrown. A police Jeep was overturned and burnt outside Ockenden's new handicapped centre in Fatima Street.

On this, her first visit to Fatima Street, Joyce was greeted with bear-hugs by Lan, Minh, Ngoc, Kim Chi and Thuy, and made especially welcome by Binh, an endearing little spastic girl with a huge grin. The children shrieked with laughter when *Ba Noë* fell off the plank bridge into the sewer and gingerly stepped through the dirty water in her high heels.

The Ockenden team held a hallowe'en party and invited the Ky Dong Street sentry inside to "bob" for apples and eat spicy buns. The children sang songs, together and individually, their voices drowning the far-away sound of guns.

The situations of some poor families had been transformed by a little love and attention from the Save the Children Fund and Ockenden. One woman Joyce met had been saved from poisoning herself and her three children after her husband lost his job. Many of the families — one with twelve children, almost all of whom had measles— lived in small bamboo huts over sewers. Another contained four children and a blind grandmother. Joyce felt particular sympathy for the eldest girl in this last family, who so longed to go to school.

It was to such poor families that a Dr Wang ministered, free of charge, every morning before his regular clinic at ten o'clock. With words tumbling out so fast that she could hardly understand him, Dr Wang eagerly told Joyce of his plan to turn the top floor of the local Rotary building into a day care and play centre. She promised that the Ockenden team would work out what was needed, plan the kitchen, organise the cooking arrangements and run the play group. The Saigon Rotarians agreed to supply the food and be responsible for lighting, heating and repairs for three years, by which time the centre should be running efficiently and would be handed over to the Government. Joyce rushed out to buy bright paint for the play group furniture.

Joyce's visit to Saigon was a tonic for the tiny Ockenden team. Even the severe inconveniences they endured seemed amusing as they described them to her. Her loving, wholehearted determination to help the Vietnamese reinforced their willingness to continue caring for families and children, in conditions of utmost hardship, for almost no money. She appreciated how cut off they felt when, after just a few days in Saigon, desperate for news from Woking, having collected a letter from Ruth, she found herself tearing it open in the street. She sat up half the night with the British volunteers, listening to their thoughts and stories and talking over their plans for the future.

Before Joyce returned to England, the staff organised a day trip for the children, to a fishing village. Paddling in the sea, Joyce felt they could be in a slightly run–down English south coast resort, were it not for small Buddhist temples on the islands in the cove.

As she prepared to leave Saigon, she was in increasingly optimistic mood, taking time off to be driven to the dressmaker's in a "cyclo", a kind of pram propelled from behind by bicycle, and measured for a blouse and skirt. She was looking forward to conveying to Geneva the news that South Vietnamese voluntary agencies would welcome UNHCR involvement in a resettlement and technical training programme.

Six months later, Saigon fell.

As the fall of Saigon became imminent, the Foreign Office instructed The Ockenden Venture to remove its British staff. Joyce was distraught. Everyone expected a blood-bath in the city. What would happen to Ockenden's handicapped children in Fatima Street? She could not convince the Home Office of the importance of letting the orphans come on the Embassy plane or with the Ockenden team. All officials would say was, "We cannot differentiate between Vietnamese children."

Then she took a call from the Home Office. The *Daily Mail* was proposing to airlift to England up to 300 Vietnamese children for whom adoption proceedings had already started. She agreed to take responsibility for them. Renée Beach prepared to fly out on the pick-up plane. Then an American airliner on Operation Babylift crashed on leaving Saigon airport. Sabotage was suspected and the *Daily Mail* flight cancelled. Then sabotage was ruled out and the *Daily Mail* plane took off.

Rex Hunt, British Consul-General in Saigon, was co-ordinating the collection of children. When news had got out about the *Daily Mail* flight, he had been besieged with pleas for help by the Dominican Sisters, the American Vietnamese Children's Fund, the Catholic Relief Society and local children's workers, as well as Ockenden. He had picked up as many children as he could, ninety-nine in all, and travelled by coach with them and Embassy officials and reporters to the airport, only to be halted at the perimeter fence. Vietnamese officials announced that the quota of 1500 children allowed by the Government to leave the country had already been filled. No more could go.

As Mr. Hunt telephoned the Ministry of the Interior, the temperature in the coaches soared. A spastic child was rushed into the airport to be hosed down. It was 110 degrees in the British Midland plane on the tarmac, yet no one was allowed to get out, not even Renée Beach, desperate to know if "her" children were on the coaches.

Three hours later, permission came for the coaches to approach the plane. By this time, the children were so dehydrated it was obvious the miniature operating theatre and intravenous drips inside the aircraft would be needed. Even when everyone was on board, officials countermanded the Government's permission for the plane to depart. Once more Mr. Hunt took to the telephone.

Forms were, at last, signed and countersigned. The plane took off. The air-conditioning began to work. Nurses and stewards (stewardesses had not been allowed on the flight because of the danger of anti-aircraft fire) began changing clothes and nappies and feeding babies. Volunteer doctors began medical checks. Many children were so sick that at least six of them would have died within three hours, if they had been left in Saigon. Some had psychological disorders after surviving the crash of the American jet. Many had scabies, two had pneumonia and one septicaemia.

Meanwhile the phone at "Keffolds" was ringing with offers of help. Vans, lorries and cars were rolling up the drive, full of clothes and shoes from schools, colleges, churches and clubs all over England. Rotarians cleared and decorated a large room at "Keffolds" to act as a nursery, then asked Joyce what furniture they should put into it. "Would you like to go and have a cup of tea first?" she stalled, realising that she had never given a thought to cots. Even before the Rotarians had finished tea, a call came to say that a van load of cots was on its way from Chicester.

Joyce joined Diane Worsley, members of the St John Ambulance Brigade and Haslemere men and women waiting in the VIP lounge at Heathrow, as one sick child after another was carried in. Then, just as Joyce saw Minh, Diane spotted Lan. They grabbed the two children, almost shaking them as they asked, "Are the others here?" "Yes," they said. All Ockenden's handicapped children were safe.

Twenty-nine children from the flight were so ill that they had to be taken to hospital where three of them died from bronchial pneumonia. The rest were wrapped in blankets, driven through the snowy night, in large airport coaches, to Haslemere, then transferred to smaller vans and cars to negotiate the narrow country lane to "Keffolds."

Inside "Keffolds," Haslemere Ladies' Circle, the WRVS, the Red Cross and St John Ambulance Brigade, reporters and cameramen, took over caring for the children, all of whom were in bed by three o'clock in the morning. A few hours later, they were awake again, smiling, laughing and holding out their hands to be noticed. One little boy, in dark tights much too long for him, wandered happily about in a pale pink dressing gown, holding a giant white and orange duck.

Since the Ockenden staff and most of the local helpers caught infections from the children, for a while specialist agency staff had to be recruited. Prospective parents waited while the Home Office sorted out papers for children with names such as Little Swan, Pretty Flying Bird, or Duong Tho Thong (Sweet Gentle Flower). Some children could not be identified, the papers for one saying only, "Small child with red anorak." Numbers which had been written on babies' hands had been sweated off during the night.

Some of the adoptions seemed happy arrangements, with families sensitive to the children's needs. Other adoptive parents were more conscious of their own needs. Joyce was powerless to prevent a three-year-old girl being torn screaming away from her two-year-old brother from whom she had been inseparable. She managed to reunite the children later, but not before they had become silent and withdrawn.

While new experiences flooded into their lives, it was safer for the Vietnamese children to stay together. They had to learn to use knives and forks instead of dipping chopsticks into a central bowl; to have meals at home rather than buying food from a stall to consume in the street. They were afraid of baths, having seen only showers, and found it strange to feel carpet under their feet, and to experience central heating. At night, unused to sleeping in separate beds, they were lonely and frightened, terrified of ghosts in which all of them believed. Being cut off from their own games and having attempts made to change their religion could make them deeply insecure. Even a creative kind of education, so different from the disciplinary one they had known, could be disturbing.

Ockenden remained financially responsible for the Vietnamese till some other legal arrangement was made. Thirteen handicapped children, including loving, intelligent Binh who had welcomed Joyce to Fatima Street, were looked after at "Kilmore" in Camberley. They became completely healthy, apart from their handicap, and retained their original personalities, not in the least disturbed by having been transported from the other side of the world.

The children were able to talk about Vietnam with two Vietnamese ladies, Ba Tu and Ba Ba, and with Renée Beach, the first administrator of "Kilmore," who would often have a group chattering and laughing in the kitchen as they buttered bread or made cakes. Seeing the medical and educational care provided, a DHSS visitor commented that no individual family could have given such personal attention. Five or six of the children would need permanent support. Four others were so mentally and physically handicapped that they would always live together in a special unit.

Only some older boys from the airlift suffered violent culture shock, becoming so unco-operative and aggressive that social workers advised separating them. Joyce disagreed, insisting on their living together with her at "Keffolds," where she could give them maximum support. She and they went through some difficult and traumatic months before she established a relationship of trust with the natural leader. Then all of them came to respect her. They began to interact naturally, learned English, went to English schools, then, as adolescents, took up independent lives, each identifying a congenial career.

Kim Chi, Ngoc, Minh, Thuy and Lan, the "famous five" as they had come to be called, lived at "Keffolds" too. Having no reason now to keep to a separate wing, they integrated with the other refugees. Mr Baikie restored their condition to what it had been before they returned to Saigon. After he retired, as refugees they were entitled to help under the National Health Scheme.

All five went to school, then to college or to a YTS scheme. Lan, who headed a team of seamstresses on Canvey Island, became engaged to a young Englishman and made her own Vietnamese-style wedding dress — long, flowing and white, with a hooped skirt. The others, bridesmaids in pink, were escorted to the wedding by police when their mini-bus lost its way. All subsequently became aunts to Lan's children, Marika and Luke.

Proof of the five's readjustment came after a visit to *Miss Saigon*, which had been arranged for children of the airlift by courtesy of Cameron Mackintosh, the producer. Diane Worsley and Denise Moll, who escorted them, were moved to tears by the story of a Vietnamese girl who gave up her child so that he could have an improved standard of living with his father in America. They wondered if they had been wise to bring the children. They need not have worried. All five bounced out in the highest of spirits saying, "Oh, wasn't that terrific!"

17   Ockenden's Second Great Blossoming

The fall of Saigon was not followed by the expected blood–bath. The puritanical North Vietnamese imposed punishments and executions for crime and corruption but considered America responsible for the war. Soon though, communism tightened its hold. Heads of families were sent to "re–education" camps: homes, money and possessions were seized. Bustling markets became deserted and cloth, rice, meat and vegetables were rationed. After thirty years' conflict, Vietnam's economy had collapsed. Now too, China cut off aid.

In 1975, news broke of a trickle of "boat people" escaping to Thailand and Malaysia. The British Government accepted 150, who had been taken to Hong Kong after a Danish trawler had plucked them off a sinking boat in the South China Sea.

Just before Christmas, thirty-six men and boys from the group arrived at "Keffolds." None had experienced normal life without war. Ken Carnac, a young teacher, taught them English, coaxing them into Haslemere's youth clubs and discos, giving them confidence to formulate what they wanted to do with their lives. Some moved into London hostels and looked for jobs. Several were accepted on training schemes. Others enrolled at technical colleges.

In 1976, the threat of an emergency increased. Vietnamese fisher folk, unable to accept restrictions imposed on their trade, began to escape to Thailand in their own boats, ending up in shanty towns or Laem Sing Camp on the coast, cared for by UNHCR. Joyce went to Thailand in May 1977, to explore the possibility of Ockenden's promoting Vietnamese settlements in South East Asia and to interview some younger Vietnamese for resettlement in England.

By the summer of 1978, more and more desperate families were escaping. Joyce met the seven unaccompanied Nguyen children at Heathrow Airport whose father and mother had been left behind while organising the escape of sixty-two families. Their sea captain had panicked, setting sail before everyone was on board. Joyce found sponsors for all the Nguyens, so that she could keep them together at "Keffolds."

New controls and taxes in South Vietnam affected, in particular, the ethnic Chinese — the traders of South East Asia — by removing incentives for private enterprise. Business people, who were urged to leave when they could not adapt to becoming agricultural workers, became prey to extortion by local officials in charge of exit visas and blackmailed by sea captains.

Most Vietnamese escaped illegally, in unseaworthy boats, through storms and rough seas in which, it is thought, 250,000 drowned. Thousands more were murdered, attacked or raped by pirates. Increasingly numerous survivors began to be turned away, towed out to sea again, or fired upon by ports which had previously accepted refugees. Soon, in the whole of South East Asia, only the small British Colony of Hong Kong allowed Vietnamese ashore.

In January 1979, the Labour Government agreed to admit 1,500 Vietnamese into Britain. By September, 60,000 more refugees were caged like impounded animals in Hong Kong camps, living on six feet by four feet metal platforms stacked on iron tiers, one platform per family.

Joyce made broadcasts about the overcrowding and lack of privacy in the camps she visited, begging the British Government and non-governmental agencies to do something about it. To no avail. Britain was obsessed with its own problems. "I sometimes wonder what they are," she said bitterly, "No one is starving in Britain. No one of good will is confined. There is no one who could not apply for welfare assistance."

The new British Conservative Government came into power with a restrictive statement on immigration, in response to public fear of a fall in the standard of living if too many less fortunate people were allowed to share it. Yet after her election, Mrs Thatcher, the new Prime Minister, quoted the prayer of St. Francis:

> Where there is discord, may we bring harmony.
> Where there is error, may we bring truth.
> Where there is doubt, may we bring faith.
> And where there is despair, may we bring hope.

To Joyce it seemed that, at that moment, Mrs Thatcher invoked the energy of compassion. Within days, British captains of the Sibonga and the Roachbank had picked up 15,000 boat people. Voluntary agencies, including Ockenden, with the full support of the media, were insisting they be allowed into Britain. Public opinion changed. Both boat loads were accepted and Lord Carrington, Britain's Foreign Secretary, went to see the situation in Hong Kong for himself. Mrs Thatcher called for a UN conference in Geneva to debate the problem of the boat people. As a result, for the first time ever, in July 1979, the UN held a conference on a purely humanitarian matter.

Before acting as an observer at the conference, Joyce represented the British Standing Conference on Refugees at a meeting of the International Council of Voluntary agencies, involving over fifty international and national agencies working to help Indo–Chinese refugees. At the end of the meeting, the President, himself a Polish refugee, read out an Affirmation which the Council sent to every government:

> "Our millions of constituents demand that we be concerned about people, not politics, about salvaging lives, not placing guilt. Those we represent want an immediate humanitarian response. This is a time for greatness of the spirit, a time to extend the horizons of our abilities, a time for governments to give assurance that the world human family will be permitted and enabled to meet its responsiblities, each to the other."

The Pope focussed his prayers and the Dalai Lama concentrated his thoughts on the UN conference, at which representatives of 72 nations came together. Sufficient help was pledged to rescue all refugees who had already left Vietnam. The British Government agreed to take 10,000 Hong Kong refugees, asking The Ockenden Venture, the British Council for Aid to Refugees and Save the Children Fund to each take responsibility for the resettlement of Vietnamese in a geographical third of the country. Ockenden's area included the Midlands, the North West, the North East, North Wales, Surrey and Gosport and the Portsmouth area of Hampshire.

Maureen Repassy, who had been Ockenden's general secretary during World Refugee Year, returned to help run the huge, Government-funded refugee programme. The Ockenden Venture, hitherto a voluntary and semi-voluntary organisation, would now also need many salaried staff. Would this weaken Ockenden's vision of a sharing world?

In the event, long-term Ockenden staff moved into positions of special responsibility, continuing to work round-the-clock. Greater numbers of salaried staff worked with equal dedication, the majority for £17 a week. Spasmodic protests from staff with families to keep received scant sympathy. Living at the simplest level herself, Joyce could not see how Westerners could expect a high standard of living on money that had been donated for refugees. Even Ockenden's salaried workers chose an alternative life-style and worked for an ideal.

Between 1977 and 1980, Ockenden created 1,000 reception places, with an explosion of twenty-five new centres loaned, donated or rented. It resettled 3,000 boat people. Until March 1982 the chief transit centre was Nelson Hall near Stafford, with 400 places, through which, by February 1982, 2,046 refugees had passed. Without its huge area of ramshackle Nissen huts, formerly a teachers' training college, resettlement would have been interminable.

In summer, the heat in Nelson Hall's thin-walled Nissen huts became unbearable. Chris Rounthwaite, Nelson Hall's administrator, recently returned from consular service abroad, knew that in winter, conditions would be even worse. Yet circumstances forced Joyce to keep the centre open.

In the particularly severe winter of 1981, with 25 degrees of frost, the pipes burst, the old-fashioned boilers broke down and the electricity supply failed. The staff, continually having to confiscate dangerous parafin stoves, were at breaking point after a spate of complaints and distress calls.

In the worst of the snow, The Ockenden Venture evacuated 160 of the most vulnerable adults and babies from Nelson Hall to houses in Birmingham, many of which were provided by Father Fallon. Alisoun Browne, who became a central pillar of the Ockenden Venture, ran one such home, years in the theatrical world having prepared her for working with temperamental people! Many other refugees barricaded themselves in, refusing to move from their first secure home. When groups from different parts of Vietnam were not fighting each other or young men flashing their knives, the atmosphere was extremely friendly. The refugees had to be reminded that Nelson Hall was a transit centre — not a Vietnamese village!

Violence was understandable among teenagers disorientated by war, then transported overseas in hardship and terror. Joan Leadley, who had worked with Poles and Hungarians at "The Abbey" and Donington Hall and had succeeded Chris Rounthwaite as administrator, had talks with the Manpower Services Commission. As a result, The Dragon Project evolved, providing employment for sixteen- to nineteen-year-olds and putting them into contact with the local community.

The Dragon's fiery breath kept essential services alive during the freezing winter, refurbished accommodation blocks and furnished a nursery. Under the guidance of Martin Bolderston, the young Vietnamese renovated church doors, cottages and cassocks, packed supplies for Poland and made bunting for a Royal Wedding celebration. Transforming the dereliction of vandalism and decay into a pleasant environment, they converted a terrace of houses in Stafford into a reception centre.

The Dragon staff, from very different backgrounds, experts and perfectionists in their own fields, measured up to the Ockenden ethos of energy, flexibility and commitment to the education of the young.

Three months after the programme started, continuing for ten years until long after the Vietnamese had ceased to need basic training, The Dragon offered literacy, horticulture, carpentry, vehicle maintenance, construction and catering courses to non-Vietnamese — difficult, disorientated and disadvantaged teenagers of all races and religions from the Potteries and Stafford. Joyce's heart went out to them, for they were no less frustrated than the young, exiled Vietnamese had been. They were, she realised "so far outside the structures of our society as not to be so much 'anti-establishment' as failing to realise that any establishment or social structures exist."

Joyce had already initiated two projects at "Quartermaine" in Haslemere for these "refugees within," as she called them. Margaret Dixon and Eric Jones were running a mid-week Care and Alternative Education and Training programme for delinquent boys, who were referred to them by Social Service authorities, and monthly weekend preventative courses for London children, taking groups of eight at a time.

For seventeen years, until Southwark Council was "rate-capped" and withdrew its grant, young Ockenden teachers and youth workers, working closely with families and social workers, were also running a neighbourhood Intermediate Treatment project for London children in Peckham. Fifty school refusers or children "at risk," all with emotional, social or educational problems, were encouraged to develop their interests and capabilities, spending every sixth weekend camping or in an Ockenden country house.

Meanwhile, the Vietnamese programme continued. Smaller reception centres, such as those in Stockton-on-Tees, Weatherby and Exmouth, whose administrators knew all their twenty or thirty refugees personally, became integrated communities, members communicating with one another in a voluble, sometimes explosive mixture of Vietnamese, English and Chinese.

Yeshe Tsultrim, the Tibetan who later opened Ockenden's Cambridge Tibetan cultural centre, was the calm administrator of the Harrogate house, where lived part of a group of 210 Vietnamese rescued after four days and nights in a small boat, without food, water or toilets. Having been ignored by eighteen passing boats, they had felt "life come again" when a British trawler had picked them up. None regretted having taken such a risk. They said, "It is better to die only one day than to die every day." Tables in the Harrogate house were permanently laid with rice bowls and chopsicks, teams of Vietnamese taking turns to cook bite-sized pieces of meat and finely chopped vegetables, mounds of rice, stuffed sweet pastries with savoury meat mixtures and dishes spiced with ginger, chilli sauce and vinegar. For special occasions, they prepared fish maw soup made from a large fish's stomach and maiden's hair sauce made from seaweed.

Education was the key to adaptation and integration. Four hours a day was usually enough, backed up by communication with local support groups. For illiterate or half-educated teenagers, for whom English seemed an insuperable barrier, Hilary Adair, a teacher of English as a foreign language, set up residential language and skills courses at "Quartermaine"— a suitable location, for 100 Vietnamese had already joined the "Quartermaine," "Keffolds" and "Coomb Head" community. The courses, characterised by hard work, cheerfulness and laughter, had a long waiting list. Many splendid teachers worked with Hilary, including Marilyn Trow who continued after Hilary left.

When it became obvious that basic skills were not enough to secure employment during a recession, courses widened to include typing and creative initiatives such as jewelry-making and house maintenance. Ockenden opened a teaching and training centre at the former North Allington Hospital in Dorset and a boarding school at Bridport, where, in the evenings and at weekends, local families offered hospitality.

There began to be hundreds of success stories. Many Vietnamese qualified for school and university. Many started businesses, including restaurants, health shops and a designer ski suit and children's clothes co-operative in Chichester. With the proceeds of a jumble sale, two fishermen bought a twelve-foot boat and constructed a fishing net in the front room of their council house. Other refugees cornered the market in unpopular jobs such as chicken-plucking or cleaning the floors of Chinese restaurants.

Ockenden's resettlement target was three months per family. The average resettlement time actually achieved by Ockenden's Barry Denton and his staff was six months. Families were placed close together for mutual support, avoiding large concentrations, which could cause local antagonism. Even so, many Vietnamese refugees suffered racial abuse, especially if they were given local authority housing in places with waiting lists. Since they were particularly at risk in grim tower blocks, they were put, whenever possible, into safer, newer developments. When local authority housing ran out, local investment trusts took over, buying houses for families whose many wage earners could usually soon repay the loans.

For the few English people who acted aggressively towards the Vietnamese, thousands treated them generously. The backbone of the resettlement process was the amazing phenomenon of support groups, 213 springing up in Ockenden's area alone. Joyce wrote, "Never in Britain's history has there ever been a grass roots community operation of quite this nature. There has been so much more that is positive than negative in all that has happened."

Ockenden in Birmingham's magazine, *Venturer*, was a focus for discussion and information between support groups. It also brought the refugees news of friends in England and in camps in Asia and invited them to meet each other at Ockenden's annual Open Day and fête. It explained Vietnamese customs and problems to English people: the grief Vietnamese parents felt when children who had to interpret for them ceased to show them filial respect; the pain and frustration when daughters, influenced by Western ways, refused to marry the men their fathers chose.

On Merseyside, where ninety five per cent of Vietnamese remained unemployed, initial hopefulness sometimes turned to despair. Most men found consolation in gardening. Most women settled to sewing or making up goods at home, though in this they were mercilessly exploited. Adults were usually happy enough if their children were making friends and progressing at school.

Having lived through a civil war, most Vietnamese knew well enough how to cope with stress. If they were single as well as unemployed, however, they could suffer from headaches, stomach upsets and depression. Their troubles were compounded when psychiatrists could not understand what they said. A stress centre which Joyce set up for them in Bridport, with professional Vietnamese consultants, produced remarkable recoveries.

By the end of 1981, 5,000 Vietnamese had been resettled in Britain. "Compassion fatigue" crept in. The West stopped welcoming boat people. "How *dare* we have 'compassion fatigue'," asked Joyce, "when we have endless compassion offered to us?" Reception centres closed. Staff whom Ockenden had recruited, whose lives had revolved round refugees, had to leave. By 1982, though there was still a steady flow of Vietnamese refugees, Ockenden's official reception programme had ended.

After the Vietnamese era, The Ockenden Venture would never be quite the same again. Still a small organisation, with a nucleus of dedicated, semi-voluntary staff inspired by Joyce's vision, it was now, and would in future, be more closely associated with the Home Office. It was given responsibility for coordinating the resettlement of boat people rescued by British sea captains and of Vietnamese admitted under the Geneva agreement to accept ten or more handicapped refugees every year.

On the ground floor of "Quartermaine," with English skills lessons loudly carried on over their heads, Eric Jones and Margaret Dixon dealt with paper work for family reunions, until, after Eric's death, Margaret Kemp did the job single-handed. The work was crucial. No Vietnamese family could settle happily in England if they had left relatives behind. Margaret and Eric liaised with UNHCR, the Intergovernmental Committee for Emigration and the Home Office, "calling up" refugees from Vietnam, China or Hong Kong. Half buried under entrance and exit visas, flight details and notes of arrival procedures, Margaret wrote,"Here there is nothing to report except statistics, with which we two keep on and on."

Two most satisfying reunions were those of the seven Nguyen children with their parents, and of ninety-nine-year-old Bui Van Dong, who had been in a closed Hong Kong camp for two years, with his children and grandchildren.

Financial responsibility for new Vietnamese refugees was taken by the Home Office, though several Ockenden transit centres remained in use. In Oxford, the De la Salle Brothers offered to look after teenage boys whose parents sent them out of Hong Kong in the hope that they could find a better life. The boys, who arrived ragged and exhausted, in a matter of days responded to the non-institutional atmosphere of the De La Salle house, and to a life style that was part-English, part-Vietnamese.

Brothers Edwin McCarthy and Felix Sheenan taught the boys En-

The seven lost Nguyan children

Barrie Denton with Vietnamese refugees outside their new home

glish, helped with homework and, since there were both Catholics and Buddhists among them, took them all to church or to a Buddhist temple on alternate Sundays. The house was a magnet for Vietnamese students from Oxford University, who strummed guitars, sang Vietnamese songs, played football, tennis and squash with the younger boys and took them on the river. As the first teenagers left, they were replaced by another set of grinning, roguish boys. When older boys returned from colleges or hostels in the holidays, the friendly house bulged with sleeping bags and bodies.

After Joyce's death, in her tradition of creating caring communities, Ockenden opened a centre in Birmingham, in Hamstead Road, Hockley, to which Vietnamese refugees, as well as refugees of any other nationality, can go for information and support. Maggie Cade is its leader and inspiration.

18 Life in The Sudan

Not even close personal involvement with every stage of the resettlement of the Vietnamese made Joyce less open to the needs of people elsewhere. In 1980 she represented the British Standing Conference on Refugees at the International Conference which President Nimeiri called, in Khartoum, to help solve his country's exceptional refugee problem.

As she and other governmental and non-governmental representatives ascended to the fifth floor of Khartoum's Friendship Hall for the second session of the conference, the lift jarred to a halt. Floor 5 was in sight but at eye level. Joyce was courteously lifted up by the male delegates and helped to squeeze sideways through the gap, before swivelling to a sitting position in the corridor. She struggled to repress the laughter which was always just beneath the surface, as first her handbag appeared, then her briefcase, then, one after another, five horizontal gentlemen doing their best to look dignified.

President Nimeiri was sure the presence of the international delegates proved nations were at last beginning to understand their interdependency, even though the disparity between rich and poor countries was increasing. People were at least talking about evolving towards one, unified, harmonious world. Joyce herself was pressing for a positive movement to bring about such wholeness by breaking down divisions and sharing resources across the globe.

As far as Joyce could see, the advance of technology, which, when she was a student at Oxford, she had confidently expected would solve the world's problems, had so far benefited no more than twenty per cent of the world's peoples. Only two solutions to the problem of inequality had been tried. Firstly, after revolutions within countries, totalitarian governments had enforced a kind of sharing but introduced their own divisive systems. Secondly, the West had doled out aid, without compassion, not in a demonstration of brotherhood. As Martin Luther King remarked, it was as if the West had tossed a coin to a beggar, giving what it did not need to further its own self-interest.

Meanwhile, as the Third World struggled to keep up, conflicts arose, destroying existing political, economic and social structures, causing new government structures to be imposed. The upheaval caused by the Third World's determination to secure a greater share of material plenty threw ordinary human beings from one system to another, plunging them into fear and insecurity, making them run. Dr Albert Schweitzer's prophecy of a movement of peoples greater than any in recorded time had been fulfilled.

Over a million refugees had poured into Sudan, the largest, poorest country in Africa, from Chad, Ethiopia, Eritrea, Zaire and Uganda, with all of which countries it had a common border. Sudan also had refugees of its own, created by warfare between the Muslim north and Christian south. Yet its Government still offered asylum, even while trying to raise the standard of living of its own people.

Sudan was the most poverty-stricken country Joyce had ever seen. As she was driven along dirt roads with other well-fed Westerners, in a column of limousines, for the first time she saw hatred in the eyes of the poor. She was ashamed of being put up in Khartoum's ancient Grand Hotel, which, in keeping with Sudan's ambitious aims of economic and social development, had been modernised to five-star luxury.

Sudan was a million square miles in size, equal to the combined areas of Britain, Ireland, France, Italy, Norway, Sweden, Spain, Portugal, Belgium and Denmark. It was virtually undeveloped, its seventeen million people mostly squeezed into the Nile Valley and the Khartoum-Omdurman urban complex. Its economic problems were exacerbated by the leaping price of oil, by floods, famine and disease, as well as by political disputes and war.

The IMF had saved the Sudan from bankruptcy by insisting on

such stringent economy measures that subsidies on wheat, sugar and petrol had to be removed. While destitute refugees poured in, skilled Sudanese personnel poured out, in search of better lives in richer, Arab, oil-producing countries. The Sudan definitely needed the help of international expertise.

In the interval between the two sessions of the conference, Joyce visited refugees in the Gaderef region of East Sudan. She jolted for seven hours along 250 miles of pitted, dusty road, through barren moonscapes with patches of dry scrub and one or two isolated villages. There were few signs of life — only scattered groups of nomadic herdsmen and, beside the road, an occasional emaciated, dying camel or goat or donkey.

The camps, packed with half a million Ethiopians and Eritreans, lacked food, water, sanitation and medical care. Normally nomadic refugees told Joyce it was almost unbearable to live in a settlement — even if it was not a prison, as refugee camps were in many parts of the world. They needed skills to find work and rehabilitation programmes for the handicapped, the elderly, children and adolescents. Help must come from outside to turn settlements into communities.

At the International Conference, Joyce joined in discussion about what action the world should take. She returned to England confident that while Ockenden was too small to handle aid, it could create a model for the development of refugee communities in Eastern Sudan, providing vocational training centres, schools, clinics and self-sufficiency schemes.

With the help of VSO, Joyce appointed as Ockenden's Sudan coordinator Anne Leng, who had worked in Africa before, as adviser to the Ministry of Overseas Development in Swasiland. Anne would be followed to the Sudan by two skilled, expatriate workers. Then, gradually, Sudanese and refugees would be trained to take over.

Being The Ockenden Venture's only representative in Africa was, Anne found, worlds apart from working for a well-funded organisation such as the Ministry of Overseas Development. In Khartoum, apart from the problem of accommodation, telephones seemed a myth and supplies of water, gas, petrol and food erratic. All forms of transport constantly broke down, for the Sudan had no spare parts. Maddeningly, the new Land Rover Ockenden had sent out remained stuck on the docks, awaiting Customs clearance beside a British Embassy lorry which had been standing there for two years.

"There are many negatives in this situation," Anne wrote. "They swim in the atmosphere like mosquitoes, puncturing every thought, waking one up to scratch at their effect."

Joyce now lived at "Keffolds," her favourite Haslemere house. To her sorrow, "Ockenden" had been compulsorily purchased by Woking Council in 1970 to make way for an estate of town houses. Its beautiful trees had been cut down. From the comparative cosiness of the kitchen at "Keffolds," she replied, "I can well imagine the food shortages and difficult conditions and your thought, 'Do we really want to work in the Sudan?' The challenge and the suffering, of course, provide the answer. But you are the one who is suffering at the operational end. You must make the running or call the tune as you feel fit where you are. I only hope your health stands up to all the vicissitudes."

The Sudanese Government was making heroic efforts to settle hundreds of groups of refugees, all speaking different languages; clashing with one another, in culture, political outlook, religion, skills and social class. Refugees from country areas, accustomed to food and water shortages, did not mind living and working in primitive land settlements. They behaved like extended families, looking after their handicapped and elderly, drawn together by shared experiences. Other, urban people, crowded into towns and cities, taking up hospital beds, outnumbering Sudanese in primary schools and fighting for jobs. Potentially delinquent young men, literate and articulate but unqualified for careers, hung about the streets. Girls drifted into prostitution. Training and wage-earning projects were badly needed, both for refugees and for the Sudanese.

Impressed by the sensitivity of Anne's notes about the differing needs of different types and groups of people, the Sudanese Commissioner for Refugees asked her to survey the entire country. A delighted Joyce congratulated her. But would Ockenden be expected to fund the survey? Would UNHCR think the huge task appropriate for such a small agency?

Investigations were complicated by guerrilla activities, bombing raids and fluctuations in the groups of refugees. Many who had fled famine rather than persecution returned home, then were replaced by quite different sorts of people. Just before Christmas 1980, 8,000 fresh fugitives from Chad halted in the desert, sick, battle-wounded, without drugs, beds or bandages, shivering in night-time temperatures of ten degrees.

Anne's personal situation improved when she found a flat close to the airport. Her Land Rover was freed, thanks to her good relationship with the Government, and she discovered an Eritrean driver who spoke both Arabic and English. Correspondence and remittances from Ockenden continued to be delayed, ceasing altogether for some weeks, while the airport was undergoing repair.

When Anne finally received a letter, she learned of Joyce's alarm at the cost of the survey. The struggle to establish a bridgehead in the Sudan had exhausted most of the "seed" money raised by an Ingrid Bergman appeal, yet there was nothing concrete to show for it. "We normally start with small operational projects and build from there, gathering resources as we go. This is the difference between the voluntary agency and the governmental approach."

Anne was very tired. Her one respite from racketing around the settlements in the Land Rover had been to sit quietly on her own for a few minutes, enjoying *karkadeh*, a cool drink made from bougainvillaea petals. She was also distressed at not having personal involvement with refugees. She withdrew from the survey, leaving it to be completed by UNHCR, and began to concentrate on a specific project for Ockenden.

She and Dick Poole from VSO drew up plans for a primary school-cum–community centre in Um Ali, a rain–fed area twenty–three kilometres east of Showak, on the other side of the Atbara river. Three thousand Eritreans, who had settled there spontaneously, were constructing houses out of hessian, mats, packing cases, corrugated iron and timber, but they lacked the materials and sophisticated skills to build a school. Neither were they keen to work for nothing. Materials and contractor costs would amount to £6,000.

If the Um Ali project was ever to get off the ground, building would have to start at once. It was already the end of April. By late May, the rising waters of the Atbara would cut off Um Ali from Showak. In June, rain would turn the site into a quagmire, calling men onto the land for ploughing, planting and harvesting. Since the Sudanese authorities would not allow the project to go ahead until all the money for it was in place, Ockenden must send £6,000 immediately.

Delay, was, of course, inevitable. There was no way Joyce could quickly find such a large sum of money before work had even begun. Ockenden relied upon the bulk of funding following a project, once donors had seen that it was worthwhile.

Shelving the Um Ali project, Anne worked out a second plan with the Eritreans in Diem Korea, a suburb of Port Sudan. Ockenden would build a pre–school there, developing literacy and vocational, household and hygiene training, and set up social and recreational facilities. Joyce sent a first instalment of £5,000.

Meanwhile, Anne rented a house in Port Sudan for the Ockenden team, hardly able to wait for the arrival of Sue Dow, whom Joyce had appointed to design the school. Joyce said Sue, a young Australian civil engineer, was "sensible, flexible and mature." She had been working at

"Keffolds" for a year, absorbing the Ockenden culture. "Tell her to bring the thinnest, lightest cotton clothing she can find," Anne replied, "My neighbour's fan is broken and the temperature in her flat is 130 degrees."

Again Anne was doomed to disappointment, for the same reason as before. The Sudanese would not allow Sue into the country until the money necessary for the whole project had arrived. A first instalment of £5,000 would not do.

Taking Joyce's advice, Anne returned to England for a medical check and a rest. It turned out that her health had been so seriously undermined that it would have been madness to return to the Sudan. It was some comfort to her that she would at least be able to brief Sue Dow about Diem Korea.

Joyce eventually secured the necessary funding to clear the Port Sudan project with the Sudanese Government. At the end of the summer, Sue Dow set out for the Horn of Africa. Taking full advantage of Anne's legacy of Land Rover and driver, she travelled three hundred miles across the vast, undeveloped land to the small Ockenden base at Port Sudan.

The densely–populated part of Port Sudan, where the refugees lived, began in the centre, where there was water, electricity and the chance of rented accommodation in closely–packed, wooden houses, neatly arranged along orderly streets. It deteriorated outwards, until, on the fringe, a mass of humanity struggled to survive in timber and brushwood shacks, without power or sanitation, and people and livestock competed for contaminated water at open wells. The Government had begun the first phase of a new urban settlement which would have its own services and facilities. Sue's long–term objective would be to help the refugees make their community self–sufficient, beginning with one small project — the playschool.

By late 1982, the school was finished and had been simply equipped.

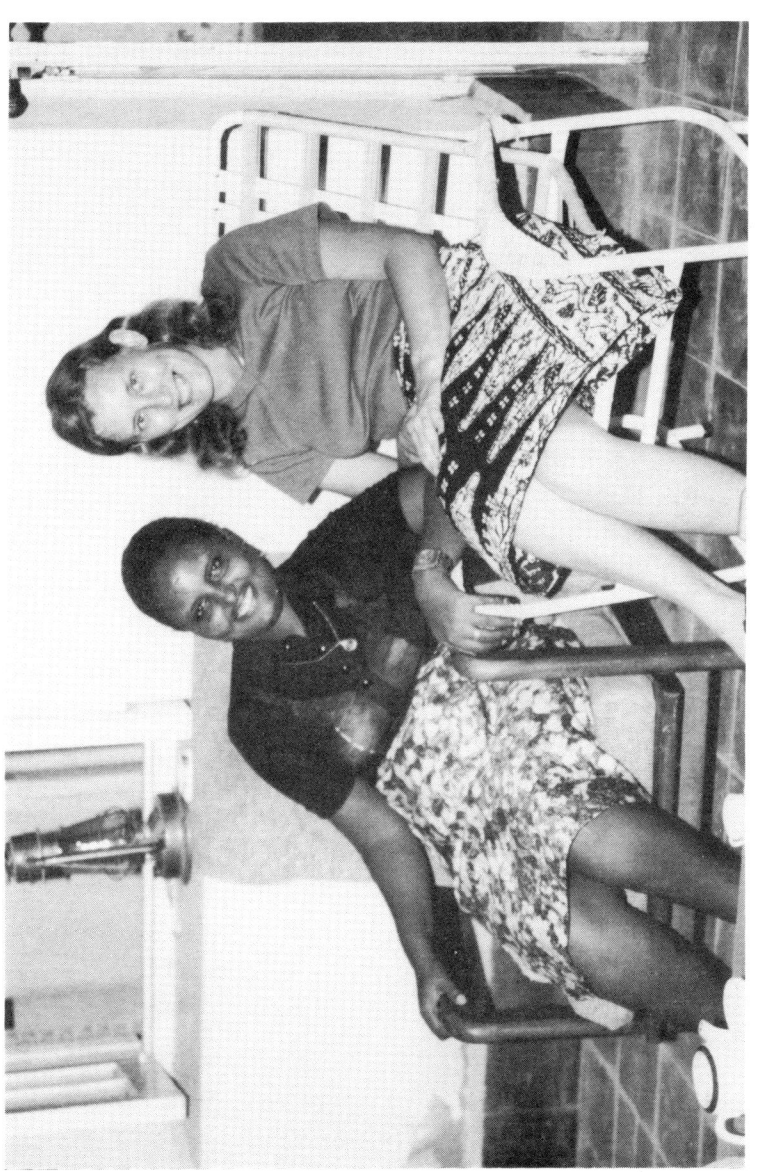

Sue Dow and friend - a rare moment of relaxation in the Sudan

Eritrean refugee children and their Eritrean teacher in Ockenden's pre-school in Port Sudan

Quietly efficient teachers were teaching sixty Ethiopian, Eritrean and Sudanese boys and girls. The school also provided supplementary food, health care and vaccinations and, in the afternoon, English lessons for refugees accepted for immigration to the United States. In addition, Ockenden obtained funds to improve some Sudanese boys' schools. Sue, who had settled down quickly and become popular with the refugees, was joined, eighteen months after her arrival, by twenty-five-year old Angela Hall, a youth and community worker seconded to Ockenden by the YMCA.

Whereas Sue was, by then, fully acclimatised to the poverty of Muslim Sudan, it appalled Angela. Dogs, goats, camels, boys and old women followed her hungrily when she went to tip out the rubbish and, as she shopped in the *souk* (market place), disabled beggars grasped at her or held out cupped hands. Yet though millions of people were dying of starvation in the Horn of Africa, the Sudanese remained hospitable, giving in their poverty to people who had nothing at all.

Simply by going to the job centre, Angela found 230 unskilled jobs and many vacancies for carpenters, builders and electricians. For the rest of the unemployed she planned skills courses and language training and sought out apprenticeships. She was always welcomed by local Sudanese companies, then invariably left sitting in an office for two or three hours, drinking hot, sweet tea and fanning the flies away, before being told, "Bukra!" (Tomorrow!). At least, for her, there was always a seat in the shade and the knowledge that, by the end of the week, something would be done. For a refugee there would be a less comfortable wait and *bukra* might not come.

Many hours spent drinking *jabina* (coffee) outside on the street with workshop owners, in the light industrial areas of Port Sudan, paid off. By the end of a year employers had offered twenty-nine apprenticeships. Ockenden paid the trainees, aged from fifteen to forty, just enough to live on, and some companies gave them breakfast, clothes and medical treatment. Soon two tailors, an electrician, a bread-seller and a photographer had been trained.

The trainees were endearingly anxious to prove themselves honest and hard-working. They were issued with Ockenden identity cards, with the result that, when a nineteen-year-old was attacked on his way home and left unable to speak, Angela was summoned to the hospital. She visited him every day, giving him food, medicine and basic care, which, in the Sudan, are the responsibility of the patients' friends and relatives. When, his condition having improved, he was expected to share his bed with another patient, she had him discharged into the care of his loving family. Then she coaxed him to talk by promising him a pound to say "thank you."

Ninety per cent of trainees completed their training successfully. With certificates to prove their qualifications, they easily found jobs. The same was true of graduates from the Ockenden secretarial courses, which, with great difficulty, Sue and Angela set up. First, typewriters failed to arrive on time, then books proved elusive. A determined Sudanese gentleman found premises for the courses, saving Sue and Angela from having to turn their home, which already acted as an office, counselling rooms and a typewriter warehouse, into a secretarial college. Sue had to teach typewriting but managed to find part-time teachers for English lessons and office practice.

When Ockenden's project in Deim Korea, which had been begun with small voluntary contributions, was seen to be successful, it drew grants from the Norwegian Refugee Council, the UN and UNHCR. Then Sue and Angela started a business loans scheme.

Handing out money to destitute people was risky. Some people made promises they had no intention of keeping. Others, particularly women, had practical skills but no business sense. Borrowers who could not repay loans were supposed to return their equipment, but some simply ran away. All the same, there seemed no alternative to offering self-help opportunities to refugees such as an old woman with school-age children to keep.

With just a little capital, most skilled men and women prospered, proud to come each week to repay their loans. They became friends, loving Sue and Angela to visit their businesses. Ockenden continued its involvement with loans until the scheme was taken over by Euro Action Accord.

By now, the *howageers* (foreign white women) were familiar Pied Piper figures in their Land Rover or on bicycles around the *souk* or *deims*, willing listeners to the familiar stories of ever-changing refugees. Local Sudanese people generously helped them in their work and invited them to family celebrations, such as two-day-long Sudanese weddings, on the second day of which, the bride performs a classical dance. They wondered why young English women without husbands or family should stay in a place where there was nothing but sun and sand; where, from the very beginning of summer, water was unavailable, except for an hour a day; where sugar, essential for true participation in the Sudanese social ritual of taking cups of tea and coffee, was unobtainable.

While most foreigners came just for financial gain, Sue and Angela were paid almost nothing. They often worked non-stop, in case, having stopped, they collapsed. When they did allow themselves to relax, they were happier drinking coffee or eating *zigni* (a traditional Eritrean dish) with refugees in their little timber shacks than drinking whisky in the expatriates' club or in the houses of rich Sudanese.

Sue and Angela supported one another, knowing that together they were far more effective than either could be on her own. Their underlying harmony, for which they frequently exclaimed, "Thank the Lord!", prevented their "divorcing" over the vexed question of who had left the top off the toothpaste tube or who had kept "clacking on the typewriter" till midnight.

Yet neither Angela nor Sue was immune from depression — about the time things took; about the incessant "Bukra, insha'Alla!" ("Tomorrow, God willing!"); about the "give me" mentality of some people and the knowledge that, for everyone for whom they found work, there were three more jobless people behind. All they could say was "Malish!" (Never mind!) They would fly to England for short holidays, then return to Port Sudan, to continue to demonstrate, in a practical way, that they cared.

Sue was refreshed by a visit to Ockenden, where she talked to people in the Woking office and "Keffolds" and, by good fortune, met the Dalai Lama. She was especially reinvigorated and inspired by Joyce. "I felt that, though I was in my corner of the world and Woking was another and Keffolds another, we were all together in one spirit. We each had a part to play, different though they might be."

After some months, a further slump in the economy of the Sudan made it necessary to transfer trainees from companies with so little work it was impossible for apprentices to learn anything. Angela developed existing connections with businesses, searched out new places and new types of position and built up evidence of the types of entrepreneurship that could succeed.

Having become established in Deim Korea, Sue and Angela were put in charge of UNHCR's refugee reception programme. The parents' committee of the boys' school found them a large house with running water to replace their primitive hut. There they interviewed the new refugees, to each of whom they could give a small cash grant and fifteen days' accommodation while they discussed the future.

One successful project for disabled men was a T-shirt business. Sue designed a timber building for the factory, with one room for sleeping in and another for working. It was encircled by a tall fence to protect the workers from the sand and rubbish that blew out of the desert. So many orders were received, from companies and from tourism, that by

1986 the business was fully independent.

On her visit to the Sudan, Joyce had been to Deim el Nour, a squatter area of Port Sudan, with Sudanese and refugees living side by side in one–room houses, without electricity and with no water running through the pipes. Lacking education and management experience, the residents had asked her if Ockenden could help them to build a social centre near the market to contribute to the development of the community.

Joyce obtained funding for building materials for the simple centre from the Norwegian Refugee Council and an agreement from ODA to pay for the construction of an adjacent pre–school. After two years' planning, with Angela organising and using Sue's designs, professional carpenters and plasterers and 398 Sudanese and Eritrean volunteers started work.

Angela had toured the *deim* on August 31st 1984, calling on everyone to attend a meeting to which, in the event, a thousand people came. With Ali, an Eritrean member of Ockenden's Port Sudan management team, conducting proceedings in Arabic, the community leaders called on young, old, skilled and unskilled refugees and locals to give one afternoon a week to build the centre. Everyone would be able to use it, they said. One of the two buildings would be used as a kindergarten in the morning, for women's activities in the afternoon, and as a social centre in the evening. The second building would have a coffee bar and toilets.

The refugees hesitated. If they ever managed to return home to their own countries, they would not reap the benefit of such hard work. In no time, though, they were swept along in a general mood of enthusiastic altruism, adopting as their motto, "Koolo Wahid" (everyone as one) — which was also a good basis on which to build up the community.

They began working on 15th September, starting in the late afternoon to avoid the mid-day sun, and laboured on by lamplight, breaking only for evening prayers. In six months they had finished. They chose a board of management from among the most active participants, which would control finance and plan social activities for everyone, even for children, women and sick people, who had not been involved in the construction.

By 1985, Ockenden's expatriate and local workers were managing eight different grass-roots projects in Port Sudan. To have developed too quickly, sending in more ex-patriates, would not only have endangered the personal involvement which was the Venture's strength but also have undermined the refugees' confidence in their own skills. The aim was to help them become independent so that, if ex-patriates ever had to leave, the projects would not disappear at the same time. In 1987, Abdel Gardir, a Sudanese, took over as Deputy Director and Programme Director for all Ockenden's Sudanese activities.

In February 1985, by which time Joyce was very ill, Lord Ennals, then chairman of Ockenden, and Mandy Smith, who had gone to work for Ockenden straight from her sixth form, went to take stock of the Sudanese schemes on Joyce's behalf, talking with the Minister of Internal Affairs, the Commissioner for Refugees and Nick Morris of UNHCR. At a Khartoum lunch party, Lord Ennals was presented with a historic sword, then there was dancing, in which the happiest, most energetic dancer was a man with one leg.

That Christmas, television had shown hundreds of thousands more refugees crossing the desert border into Sudan, fleeing war, drought and crop failure. The drought was also bringing rural Sudanese people down from the Red Sea Hills. Many agencies were importing food aid, but it was clear to Lord Ennals and Mandy that this was not a suitable role for a small organisation. Instead, The Venture would continue concentrating on developing facilities and communities.

Mandy returned home fired with determination to help Sudanese children. She raised money for the construction of a playgroup centre by talking to schools and youth clubs in her own district of the West Midlands. English youth club volunteers went to the Sudan to build it.

The team stayed in a youth hostel beside a dirty, rock–hard beach. They travelled six miles each way to the site twice a day, working a five–hour morning shift that started at 4.30 a.m., and a second shift beginning at half–past three and continuing through the lamp–lit darkness that began at five o'clock. A downpour briefly banished heat, smells and flies but created drainage problems. Goats ate the plans. Three hundred and fifty children hampered the workers by swarming over the site. A little Sudanese boy, who liked organising, lined all the children up and Ruth and Elly, two English girls, were delegated to entertain them.

In two weeks, the work was finished. The children climbed all over the climbing frame, the bridge, the high platforms and the swings. Beside the play centre, on what had been waste land and rubble, were now smooth places for volley and basket ball. Toys and equipment followed in the wake of a British television appeal by Bob Geldof.

Ockenden's work in the Sudan continued to expand, as one expatriate handed over to the next. Local people developed management skills, some coming to England for extra training. When Joyce died and Ockenden thought it necessary to appoint four people to cope with all the work she had been doing, Jim Thomson, the new overseas director, sent John Stops, a youth and community worker from Cardiff, to the Sudan.

John was astonished by what he found. He said no one in the Woking Office could have any idea how well Ockenden's Sudanese programme had developed; the quality of relationships that made it so special; the feeling of family alive and well, supporting everyone, despite their sense of loss. The success was due to strict observance of

Joyce's rule that the team should never, ever, be tempted to think that they knew best. They should have the humility to listen, to respond, with respect, friendship and down–to–earth practicality to the initiatives refugees and local people put forward.

19 An Ashram in East Bengal

In 1971, Ockenden's twentieth year, another appalling refugee crisis was created. East Pakistan fought for independence from West Pakistan and became Bangla Desh — the Bengal nation. The month-long conflict killed millions of people, destroyed crops, bridges, factories and homes and obliterated whole towns.

When the fighting subsided, Joyce, keen to help a few of the unimaginable numbers of newly orphaned children, learned from David Ennals that a Hindu lady, Mrs Maitreye Devi, was sheltering some Bangladeshi children in north-east India.

Maitreye Devi had been influenced both by the pacifist ideal of Mahatma Gandhi and the spiritual teachings of Rabindranath Tagore, the Hindu philosopher-poet, whose pupil she had been. Tagore, who lived as simply as Gandhi, passed on to Mrs Devi his love of children and his awareness of God at the heart of a beautiful universe.

Now, in middle age, Mrs Devi saw her country torn apart by political strife and religious fanaticism. Clashes between hostile communities were turning it into a tottering carriage, all wheels of which were loose and threatening to break away.

Just as revelations about the German concentration camps and the explosions at Hiroshima and Nagaski had changed the course of Joyce's life, so, one January night in 1964, there came a turning point for Mrs Devi. From her verandah, she saw twenty-three homes on fire and heard the screams of families trapped inside. It had been rumoured that a sacred relic — a hair of the prophet Mohammed — had been stolen. As a result, all over India men, women and children were dying. From that night on, Mrs Devi set herself to combat religious fanaticism.

Ordinary Hindus and Muslims in Mrs Devi's neighbourhood of East Bengal, sickened by the carnage, were only too eager to help her break down suspicion by forming an inter-community association based on friendliness and common sense.

The Council for the Promotion of Communal Harmony (CPCH) was founded on 30th January 1965, the sixteenth anniversary of Gandhi's assassination. It organised gatherings of Hindus and Muslims, who had never before met socially, drew Muslim women out of their compounds for education, and published the work of Muslim intellectuals for Hindus to read. Monitoring vernacular newspapers for any sign of religious provocation, it disseminated the peaceful teachings of Tagore and Gandhi throughout India, trying especially to reach the minds of children.

In March 1971, ten million Bangladeshis fled their country, where men were being killed in battle and women and children herded into groups and shot. CPCH set up a medical centre at the border by the Kapotaksha river, providing first-aid, innoculations, medicines, water bottles and petrol. As the Bangladeshis were put into camps, CPCH organised classes, meetings, schools and handicraft projects for them.

When the war was over, the Bangladeshis surged home. Mrs Devi took some orphans back to Bangladesh, where she set up an orphanage called "Khelaghar" (playschool), in a travellers' overnight hostel in Jessore.

There David Ennals met her while he was on a UN mission to help Bihari people caught in the crossfire between East and West Pakistan. The Biharis, having been victimised as Muslims in India, had gone to live in the non-secular Muslim state of East Pakistan, only to find, when it became Bangladesh, that they were again the objects of hostility, this time because they had cooperated with the former West Pakistan-controlled Government. They had to live in open sewer-like camps with one tap for 10,000 people and daily rations of an ounce of grain, a little sugar and some dried milk.

In this desert of racial hatred, Mrs Devi's orphanage, refusing to distinguish between children who needed help, was an oasis of sanity.

David Ennals suggested to Joyce that Ockenden might support Khelaghar. "Mrs Devi is in her late fifties, an inspiring, dedicated woman (I told her that you possess the same qualities as herself), greatly admired by all who know her in India and Bangladesh and held in great respect by Indira Gandhi."

Khelaghar had no official funding, for the Bangladesh Government was too preoccupied with creating a new state and repairing flood and war damage to have time to look at the situation of children. Joyce sent £500 and, with the help of photographs of the children and their pitifully short case histories, found fifty British sponsors.

The Ockenden sponsorships eased Mrs Devi's financial problems without solving them. Only her fighting spirit kept Khelaghar alive. Finally, finding adoptive parents for some children, she took the remaining fifteen boys back to India. Ockenden sponsorships followed, increasing in number as local Indian children joined a brand new Khelaghar, near Badu, a backward Muslim village in East Bengal.

At last Mrs Devi could create an environment in which children from conflicting communities could grow up peacefully together. She put into practice educational theories based on Santiniketan, Tagore's famous non-institutional school, combining academic learning with vocational training.

Lessons were taught out of doors so that, unrestricted by desks or chairs, the children would imbibe education like light or air. Spirits were uplifted and imaginations stirred by dance, music and poetry, and, in particular, by the songs of Tagore who had won the Nobel Prize for Literature. As Khelaghar became well-known, poets, artists, musicians and scholars willingly made the twenty-three-mile journey to Badu from Calcutta to give lessons.

The first fifteen boys lived in tents in a grove of mango trees and heavy jungle. As the jungle was cleared, a village quickly grew up, in a two-acre compound. Its thatched huts, with wide verandahs to provide shelter from monsoon rains, were surrounded by gardens.

Under the largest mango tree, a raised concrete platform was built for dancing, meetings, singing and music. Several smaller thatched platforms were constructed for lessons and Ockenden paid for two brick dormitories, called *Nest* (need) and *Chhayatal* (under the shade). A brick-built kitchen replaced a bamboo and thatch one.

Soon Khelaghar overflowed with children from Bangladesh and from Calcutta, to whose 150 million poorest people in the world a million unemployable refugees had been added after partition had wrecked the economy of much of Bengal. The children, physically and mentally exhausted by poverty and war, in the stable atmosphere of Khelaghar began to grow happy and healthy, developing individual personalities and gifts.

Because they were not incited to racial or religious intolerance, Muslims, Hindus, Charmor and Brahmin children saw no reason not to become a natural, unified family. Mrs Devi did not want to break down their faiths or to substitute irreligion for religion, but to liberate them from the obsolete, superstitious practices clung to by the opposing communities. Instead of starting the day with separate forms of worship, they began by singing together Tagore's hymn to truth,

> Jay jaya satyer joy (We shall dedicate ourselves to truth today)

Tagore's songs helped the children understand that having a religion did not mean that you could secure special privileges, jobs, land or power, but that you had a personal relationship with God.

Whether in the dairy or the poultry farms or on the land, work was an integral part of the children's lives. They even sang one of Tagore's songs as they went about it: "Our work and play are just the same."

The farm benefited the village, for the villagers shared the school's craft centre and the expertise of volunteer instructors such as Ockenden's Tony Beck. They used the kiln for making pottery, the hand looms for weaving saris, carpets and bed covers, and the carpentry facilities for making furniture from timber and bamboo. Products made by the children and the villagers were sold locally and in Calcutta.

Khelaghar pupils, neatly dressed, confident and friendly, became famous in Calcutta. Because of their late start, not many reached university, though a large number excelled in music, dance and drama. Some performed on the radio, others in Gorky Sadan, one of the most sophisticated auditoriums in Calcutta, and in the Netaji indoor stadium with a capacity of 80,000.

Khelaghar had a cultural impact on the whole neighbourhood, staging conferences to foster higher values and a spirit of social service. They were reminiscent of Joyce's sixth form conferences, involving many eminent people, especially writers, attracting as many as 600 school children at a time. Khelaghar's own children provided the entertainment, singing Tagore's songs.

On the festival of Ras Purnima, the full moon, and Basant Utsar, the spring festival or festival of colours, up to 2,000 visitors would crowd into the Khalaghar compound to celebrate the children's bond with nature. During the annual August tree-planting ceremony, a tree would be carried in procession round the campus, to the accompaniment of singing and dancing and the playing of drums and other musical instruments, halting at a flower-decorated hole in the ground. An important person, such as the Vicar of St Paul's Cathedral in Calcutta, would plant the first tree, then everyone would chant in praise of the elements — land, air, water, wind and sun — which would keep it alive. Each child would be given his or her own tree to plant, and the responsibility for looking after it.

Boys wore yellow dhotis for the ceremony, long pieces of cloth shorter than saris, tucked in at the waist. The girls wore yellow dresses. Both girls and boys had two yards of red cloth tied round their waists.

Their foreheads were smeared with sandal paste and round their necks they wore garlands of jasmine or of the yellow Kadam flowers of mythical history, which Krishna wore in his hair. When the trees had been planted, guests and villagers joined in more singing and dancing.

Khelaghar became thought of as an ashram, a place of retreat from the violence and discord of the world. Joyce agreed that Ockenden would pay for the construction of two cottage guest houses, in keeping with Tagore's idea of a meeting-place of simple village standard, where individuals who believed in spiritual unity could get in touch with one another and Westerners and Indians reach a better understanding of each other's lives.

Many Ockenden staff spent time in the ashram, including Renée Beach who found it strangely enjoyable to meet the children and see them running about, "playing and singing as they go." Joyce, who was never able to visit the guest house herself, hoped refugee children from the Third World living in Haslemere would go there one day, to remember the problems from which they had escaped but by which the majority of the world's children were still affected.

Some Khelaghar children became teachers, the first one to do so returning to the village as a weaving instructor, the second coming back to teach music. Most children became farmers, weavers or carpenters and were found accommodation with families.

Mrs Devi frequently visited Joyce, bringing videos of the children to England, trying to raise more money for more land and more sponsorships, continuing to promote Khelaghar whose motto was,

> Where the mind is without fear
> The head is held high
> And knowledge is free.

Drawing water at Khelaghar

Khelaghar - part of the spring festival

An Eritrean boy and a Vietnamese boy at "Keffolds"

20 Thai Payap

In 1978 the British began to worry about the thousands of Laotians and Kampucheans who were joining the thousands of Vietnamese fleeing overland into Thailand. As a result, so much money flowed into relief agencies, that Joyce was able to send £5,000 to Thailand. She knew that long-term, practical help was needed, if these new refugees were not to fall into a state of permanent dependency.

Even before the communist Pathet Lao took control of Laos, the country had been devastated, its Buddhist culture obliterated by rival factions supported by America and North Vietnam. Afterwards, under cover of a People's Democratic Republic, 20,000 North Vietnamese troops destroyed or expelled the Laotian middle classes, forcing Laotian citizens from their homes.

As the whole of Indo-China became united under the North Vietnamese military dictatorship, the tragic survivors of the Pol Pot regime were also driven out of Kampuchea (formerly Cambodia).

Thailand at first accepted everyone, believing that most refugees would soon be resettled elsewhere. Then the West cut immigration quotas. In any case, hearing that South East Asians were finding it hard to integrate into Western societies, the refugees thought it best to stay where they were, in a country whose culture they understood.

The Thai army began thrusting refugees back towards the borders of their own countries, where their own military shot at them. Many were blown up by mines. Despite all the United Nations Border Relief Organisation could do, thousands of refugees died of malnutrition and disease. Thousands more were imprisoned in closed camps, in Thailand's northern region.

There were many children among the refugees. A description by thirteen-year-old Ge Paoin of how it felt to be penned up in a closed camp, reached Ockenden.

"I often dream of walking away from the barbed wire, as if there were no check points or police asking for passes. In the dreams, I walk into a Thai village, where shops are full of things for sale and the smell of food tempts my palate. Then I wake up and realise that it was just a dream. I used to weep over it but I don't cry now, not for anything in the world.

"Some boys sneak into the woods and catch parrots for sale. They tie the bird's legs with little chains to prevent them flying off. It hurts me to see the chains and the barbed wire around the camp. Sometimes I have nightmares of tearing at chains around my ankles and the barbed wire, screaming and screaming till I wake up.

"I'll go anywhere to resettle, even at the risk of forsaking my father and mother. They couldn't weep for me any more, I know. We've lost so much already, no tears would be shed because of separation."

Joyce sent John Bygate, a young Englishman, to Nan, a remote, mountainous region of Northern Thailand, to head a team of UNHCR financed local and British workers who were taking over a YMCA self-help trading project and school. This was in Ban Sob Tuang camp, a sloping settlement of rough plywood, straw and bamboo huts, inhabited by 12,000 Laotians Hmong, Htin, Mien and Leu tribes.

The Hmong tribe, from the highest slopes of the mountains, were religious. Each of their houses in Laos had contained at least one altar, on which animals were sacrificed to the spirits by the village faith medium, at times of illness, birth, death or marriage.

The Htin and the Mien were hill tribes too, shy, unassertive people, speaking the dialects of the villages around which their lives had revolved. The Mien were one of twelve branches of the Yeu tribe, who, according to legend, sprang from a marriage arranged by a Chinese emperor between his daughter and a dog as a reward for the dog's noble deed.

The fourth tribe were the Leu, lowland rice farmers who came from long-established riverside communities of wooden houses, built round ancient, architecturally sophisticated temples.

John Bygate and his Ockenden team organised a vocational training programme for the refugees in Ban Sob Tuang, making it acceptable to the authorities and forging links with the local community by opening it to Thai teenagers. The courses in literacy, building, watch repairing, electronics, elementary mechanics, nutrition, baby welfare and accounts were subsidised by the training project, which drew upon the centuries-old skills of the refugees.

From the age of five, all Laotian women were assiduous embroiderers. One had even created the world by sewing land together, pulling up the mountains with her needle! Some motifs, such as that of playing kittens, were common to more than one tribe, suggesting a historical link, in particular, between the Hmong and the Mien, but each tribe had its own, distinct type of embroidery.

Mien women and girls stitched from the reverse side of the cloth. Their motifs, inspired by legend or natural and man-made forms, reflected their moods, experiences and surroundings. Hmong girls specialised in finely pleated, swishing skirts, made from six yards of indigo-dyed batik, hand-printed with broad embroidered borders. They made dazzling appliqué belts, patterned with sinuous natural shapes and eye-twisting geometrics.

The Htin and the Leu were weavers. The Htin wove silk and cotton cloth, with traditional motifs traceable in temple wall hangings in memory of relatives, in white to commemorate a natural death and in red to signify an accident. The Htin used tough strips of bamboo to weave walls, matting, posts and baskets, creating geometrical patterns with black grass.

The refugees bought high quality yarns and materials at cost price from Ockenden, then used their ingenuity to suit the market, making cushion covers, purses, baskets, bedspreads and table runners. Ockenden bought the articles for export, finding outlets in Japan, Australia, Canada, Europe and America. By the end of 1980, profits reached £75,000. Visiting Ban Sob Tuang, in the autumn, Joyce and David Ennals decided to extend the project to Nam Yau camp twelve miles away.

Joyce and David Ennals also visited Ockenden's educational, vocational and trading project for Kampucheans in Kamput camp, the director of which was Steve Salmon, a young Englishman who had been working in Thailand for four years, had married a young Thai girl, Suwadee, and had a little daughter. Steve and Suwadee arrived in August, ready to receive the first weary, depressed Kampucheans from Khaoi holding centre.

Knowing how Kampucheans loved celebrations, Steve suggested a three-day festival. The refugees threw themselves into the event, becoming a community as natural creativity triumphed over fears and memories to bring sanity back into their lives.

Slap-stick comedians materialised from nowhere. Ballet dancers appeared, former members of the Cambodian national ballet school. Woodwind and stringed instrument players trained others to perform and performed themselves.

After the festival, Steve organised a PT instructors' course for 30 young men and women who would then teach the camp's 500 children.

That autumn, Joyce and David Ennals enjoyed a cut-down version of the festival and an impressive (though, to Joyce, somewhat threateningly martial) PT display. The instructors marched forward in white T-shirts, navy shorts, gleaming white socks and running shoes, holding a streaming banner, with Olympic rings over Ockenden's early oak tree logo which recalled the house where everything began.

Changes had to be made in Ockenden's operations in Thailand, for in 1982 the Royal Thai Government decided to divide the refugees among three super camps, each for 50,000 people. One camp would

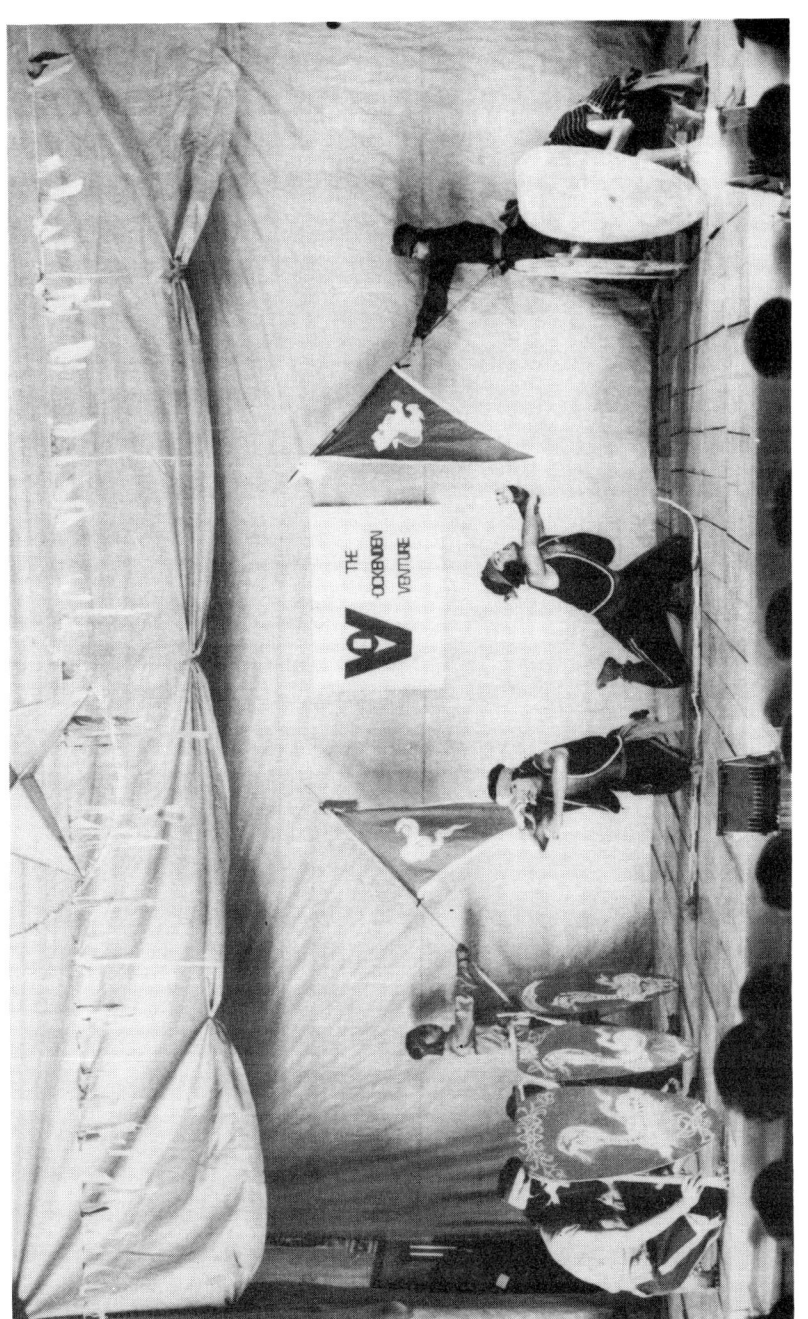

The festival at Kamput camp

Hmong women's literacy class

Mien embroidery baby carrier with baby wearing "good luck" hat with distinctive red wool pom-poms

be for the lowland Leu tribe, one for Kampucheans and one for the highland tribes, the Htin, the Mien and the Hmong. Kamput and Ban Sob Tuang were closed.

Steve, Suwadee and the rest of the Ockenden team concentrated their efforts on Nam Yao camp, the only mixed camp to remain open. They trained refugees of all tribes in management and administrative skills, in a handicraft co-operative, the Leu showing the others how to make and operate machines for deseeding cotton, carding, spinning and weaving. Then Steve developed craft production for local Thai people, in Nan's isolated mountain villages.

Fire frequently crackled through the 2,500 bamboo and thatch huts in Nam Yao, where 10,000 people were jammed close together on the hillside. The Ockenden team took responsibilty for fire-fighting and fire prevention, starting a blacksmith's forge to make fire-fighting tools. They operated a hospital in conjunction with the American Tom Dooley Heritage, and an opium addiction unit for the Hmong and the Mien, who had traditionally grown poppies for profit and medicine.

When the Thai authorities moved 7,000 hill tribe people out of Ban Nam Yao, to Ban Vinai camp nearer the Laotian border, every voluntary agency except Ockenden left Ban Nam Yao. The Ockenden Venture remained there, working with 1,200 Htins and 800 Hmong who were allowed to stay there while their claim to have been born on the Thai side of the border was investigated.

The craft project was vital for these Htin and Hmong people, who, while waiting for Thai nationality, were not entitled to subsistence rations or government services. With the income from the project they expanded their school and adult literacy centre, installed a gravity-fed, piped drinking water system from local springs, and dug out a fish pond large enough to supply everyone in the camp. Finally, they built a Buddhist temple in the middle of their new community.

Ockenden continued to operate craft programmes, with funding from the Norwegian Refugee Council and ODA, developing education and encouraging enterprises such as a bakery, with loans which were soon repaid. The craft project expanded to Thai villages and to new communities which refugees had been allowed to found in Thailand. The villagers were delighted to earn surplus money with *hattasin* (hand art), with which they could buy rice when crops were poor. The project also enabled men to work at home, instead of being obliged to travel to poorly paid labouring jobs, 200 kilometres away.

The first step towards full independence from Ockenden came when the project chose its name, "Thai Payap," meaning "North Thailand". In the dry season, when work in the fields stopped, the Ockenden team held marketing, technical and organisational seminars, always looking out for refugee and Thai leaders who would be able to take over.

Thai Payap incorporated eighteen villages, twenty-one tribal groups and 874 producers, providing incomes benefiting 5,000 people. Each village formed a production association, with an elected leader to organize raw materials, book-keeping and the steady production of top quality products. The best articles were displayed in Ockenden's showroom in Nan.

Steve expanded Ockenden's work in Ban Nam Yao camp and Ban Sob Kok village by introducing ecologically sound agricultural methods, tackling land erosion caused by deforestation, and the decrease in crops resulting from "slash and burn" cultivation. He demonstrated how to divert river flows to prevent bank erosion, and encouraged the refugees and villagers to reintroduce trees and bushes, and to begin rotation contour planting in horizontal alleys on the hillsides. He introduced new food crops of vegetables, wheat and beans to supplement hill rice and maize, and, in a nutrition improvement programme, developed goat and milk production.

As the Thai projects expanded, refugees and villagers became increasingly independent until, finally, Ockenden could withdraw altogether. In 1988, three years after Joyce's death, on the sixtieth birthday of the King of Thailand, three cotton weavers and three basket makers from Nan demonstrated *hattasin* under a Thai house in the Barbican in London. Totally at ease in a major Western arts centre, they conveyed with skill and confidence, to 16,000 visitors, the pride, informality and dignity of a Thai village.

21 The Afghans in Pakistan

In 1984, Joyce asked a young Tibetan couple, Lobsang and Yangchhen Yeshi, to give hope and practical help to at least a few of the millions of Afghan refugees in Pakistan.

The Afghans had formerly lived traditional Muslim lives in their mountainous country of brooks and rushing rivers, where birds sang in peach and apricot trees and butterflies danced over fields swaying with corn and wheat.

In 1978, the communist regime had imposed changes on Afghan society, redistributing land in favour of the poor and reforming the dowry system. However beneficial such changes might have been, so ruthlessly were they introduced that they aroused political and intellectual opposition in towns and armed resistance in the countryside.

As repression of opposition intensified, with many executions being carried out, young Muslim men were urged to become mujahadeen (freedom fighters) in a jihad or holy war. The Kabul Government then called in the Shuravi, the heavily armed forces of the Soviet Union.

In the course of mujahadeen attacks on the Shuravi, with rocket launchers and Kalashnikov rifles, and during retaliation bombing by the Russians, a million civilians died. Thousands were maimed. Farms, vineyards and irrigation channels were destoyed, mosques and schools shelled and hundreds of villages blasted into rubble.

Four million Afghans escaped westwards to Iran and south eastwards over steep mountain passes into Pakistan. There three million of them, the largest concentration of refugees anywhere in the world, halted in the arid North West Frontier.

Pakistanis took their Afghan Muslim brothers into their homes, until they were overwhelmed by the huge numbers. Pakistan kept its border open, even when the Russians attacked from the air. Locals, as well as Afghans, had to move to safer zones. Selling what possessions they had for food, the Afghans waited to be registered by the Pakistan Commissioner for Refugees, and so entitled to UNHCR rations of sugar, wheat, cooking oil and tea.

Many were disappointed. The funds donated internationally for refugees were inadequate for such unprecedented numbers. When Ockenden's chairman, Lord Ennals, visited Pakistan in 1984, he found hundreds of unregistered Afghans living on spasmodic hand–outs or on help from relatives, their situation as bleak as that of the emaciated dogs that prowled the camps.

Some men found seasonal work, such as clearing out canals, but there was no employment for women. The shabby groups of *katchas* or mud huts, where single mothers, often mujahadeen widows, lived, were identifiable by their makeshift roofs made out of untidy pieces of plastic or tarpaulin. The families of war–disabled men were equally destitute.

Many aid organisations had started projects to help Afghan families generate income. After discussion between Lord Ennals and UNHCR, it was decided that Ockenden could revive traditional skills in a quilt–making project. A soft, cotton quilt was distributed to every refugee family by UNHCR, for sleeping or sitting on, or for warmth. Surely refugees could make the quilts more cheaply than commercial producers and would have a personal interest in quality?

Joyce thought the idea would work. She asked Lobsang and Yangchhen Yeshi if they would try it out. The Yeshis, refugees themselves, were more than willing to help the Afghans for a while. They did not anticipate that it would be four years before they would return to England, and then only because Ockenden insisted it was time for them to have a change.

As stateless Tibetans, Lobsang and Yangchhen had no passports — it would have seemed a betrayal of Tibet to have taken on British nationality. It took all of six months to obtain travel documents. In

September 1984, they finally left England for Peshawar, in Pakistan's North West Frontier Province.

To the Yeshis' dismay, ex-patriates were not permitted to live in the refugee settlements, but only in the expensive, university part of town. Economising as best they could by living on toast and eggs in a small hotel, they searched for cheap accommodation. Fortunately, two Australian water drillers were pleased to share their six-bedroomed bungalow in return for Yangchhen's cooking. It only remained for Lobsang and Yangchhen to persuade UNHCR to lend them a pick-up truck, then they were ready to start visiting camps.

Nasirbagh, where the Yeshis had expected to set up their project, turned out to be a model settlement already. Liaising with other NGOs (non-governmental agencies), they found many programmes already flourishing there. They decided to begin their project in Kababian, the poorest camp of all, isolated and waterlogged, with no projects of any kind for its 19,000 inhabitants.

Since they were used to people thinking they knew best what would benefit refugees, Lobsang and Yangchhen were not overcome by surprise to hear that Westerners had started projects in Kababian and then abandoned them because they had failed. They also knew that Afghans would wonder why Tibetans should want to help them. They would probably suspect them of having an ulterior motive, such as converting them to Buddhism. Afghans obeyed Muslim laws even more strictly in Pakistan than they had done in Afghanistan, wearing their national costume of *kameez* (long top), *shalwar* (trousers, often with a band of embroidery) and scull cap or *pugree* (cloth head covering) at all times.

Yangchhen and Lobsang understood the refugees' wish to retain their Afghan identity, feeling a similar need themselves to stay positively Tibetan. They made it a priority to create an atmosphere of trust, taking a Pushtu and Persian-speaking interpreter to the camps with them. They already had the advantage of speaking, between them,

Bengali, Hindi and Urdu.

First the Yeshis went to the mosques, the most important places in the settlements, to see what the mullahs thought of their idea. Then they consulted the *maliks*, the former village leaders who still led the village groups in exile. Finally, while Lobsang talked to ordinary Afghan men, Yangchhen talked to women. The reaction was the same everywhere. How marvellous to be paid for making quilts!

The Yeshis obtained Pakistani Government permission, then had plans drawn up for a factory. Over cups of green tea, they signed an agreement for Ockenden to use a particular site, on condition that the buildings erected on it would belong to the landlord when the Afghans returned home. Then construction began. Lobsang had to order the Pakistani builders to knock the walls down and start again, not once but several times, before they accepted that it would not be possible to use sub-standard materials for refugees.

While the building work was in progress, Lobsang and Yangchhen started women off sewing quilts at home, giving them sewing machines for which they would pay in instalments out of their wages. Yangchhen decided to charge for needles and thimbles too, because (as the Afghan women agreed, with many giggles) these little objects had lives of their own.

Quilts began to arrive at the settlement store, balanced on the heads of children or pulled along in little wooden carts. Each child had a notebook in which the number of quilts he brought was recorded, so that there would be no argument at the end of the week when his mother thumb-printed her wage agreement. The Yeshis piled the quilts into their pick-up truck, taking them home to stuff into the bedrooms of their bungalow while stock accumulated.

It took courage for Afghan women, who never otherwise left their family compounds, to begin coming to the store. First to conquer her fear was Mascoma, a thirty-nine-year-old widow. Her need was great, for she had been struggling to feed herself and four children with help from relatives and the wages of her eldest son, a roadside cobbler. Mascoma's glossy hair and strong face had been uncovered when Yangchhen had first talked to her, in her *katcha*, but she arrived at the store in impenetrable disguise. She was completely concealed by a voluminous, brightly-flowered, sheet-like garment and a shuttlecock-shaped headdress with a thick veil.

Keen though she was to prove she could use a sewing machine, Mascoma's quilts were always an eccentric shape, even though Yangchhen gave her regular ten-yard lengths of cloth. Humiliatingly, a group of men sewing quilts by hand, cross-legged on the ground, were much more proficient.

Mascoma kept trying, over and over again, always having her quilts rejected, until one day she mastered the art of sewing them properly. After that, she kept returning for more cloth. She could soon buy meat for her children and a little extra food for feast days, increasing, as she did so, in confidence and dignity.

Emboldened by Mascoma's success, her young relative, Fatima, dared to walk through the camp to fetch work too, pulling her chador over her face and marching quickly past huts and tents where men from other tribes lived. Queues of other women soon followed Mascoma and Fatima's example.

Lobsang, using a magnifying instrument to count the number of threads to the square inch, checked the quality of the cotton cloth. Yangchhen taught the women to quilt in two-inch squares instead of randomly, first having floral designs printed on the cloth, to guide the lines of stitching, and letting the Afghans choose their own colours. The UNHCR commissioner who took delivery of the first quilts said they were the best he had seen.

The one-storey, flat-roofed quilt-making factory, which took up a whole acre, was finished and inaugurated by the Afghan Refugee

Handicraft project, Thailand

Afghan man fluffing out cotton

Afghan refugees with completed quilts

Commissioner in a televised ceremony in September 1985. A hundred Afghan women watched, unseen, from a curtained area set up for them by Yangchhen.

The factory gave the women the chance to chat and gossip with women from other tribes, as well as to earn more money than the average male labourer. Soon, 127 widows or wives of disabled husbands were marching bravely from their secluded compounds to the factory. Having been woken at five in the morning by the muezzin's call to prayer, they would begin quilting at seven o'clock, then, after a short break for lunch, continue until four o'clock, six days a week.

When the women went home, thirty-two men entered the factory, to card cotton, filling the air with strands of cotton fibre as they fluffed out five-kilo bales. They used an implement with a round base and a thong, beating the thong with a mallet as if playing a musical instrument. Then they filled bags, made by refugee "tailors" for the next day's quilting.

By the end of the year, the pilot scheme was a full-scale operation. Yangchhen extended it to four more camps. When UNHCR's requirement of 75,000 quilts had been met, more orders came from Shelter, International Aid and Afghan Aid.

So many people with sewing skills wanted work, that Yangchhen and Lobsang were able to start a simple tailoring project, to make the school uniforms which UNHCR gave to the Afghan boys who could go to school. Sewing machines began clicking away in Kababian, Warsak and Michi camps, as sixty refugee tailors, many disabled, began making 10,000 long shirts, 10,000 pairs of baggy trousers and school bags, and 65,000 peaked school caps. The price of the refugee-made articles was substantially lower than that of the previously commercially-made products and the quality infinitely superior. On graduating from the training the project gave him, each tailor was given a sewing machine and materials to start up on his own.

The ultimate accolade of the Yeshis' competence and resourcefulness in hiring labour and organising production was UNHCR's decision to give them responsibility for marketing all handicrafts produced in Afghan settlements and to fund a marketing centre for Ockenden in Peshawar. The centre co-ordinated sales and prices and developed market research and expertise useful to all agencies involved in income-generating projects.

The unusual, beautiful products marketed from the centre reflected the rich heritage of the Afghan tribes: the Turkman, the Hazara, the Tajik, the Pashtun and the Uzbac. There were quilted jackets and waistcoats, skirts, carpet bags, leather goods and honey from a UNHCR bee-keeping project. The centre was also an outlet for potters, tailors, shoemakers, carpenters and silversmiths. Even the most exquisite product would contain a tiny flaw, carefully placed to show that its creator was not so presumptuous as to imply perfection, thereby attracting the attention of the evil eye.

Not everyone in Peshawar was well-disposed towards refugees. To encourage good relations with the local community, the Yeshis recruited half refugee, half Pakistani staff. Even so, local hostility could be a problem. Yangchhen was paralysed with fear when someone pointed out a bomb (defused, though she did not know it) in the garden of the centre, just near the pram in which Tensing, her baby boy, was sleeping.

All the same, there was much to celebrate when Lord and Lady Ennals spent Tibetan New Year with the Yeshis. The four passed a shining apple from one to the other, submitting their hopes for the year ahead. Then they placed it on a table shrine on which were butter lamps and a photograph of the Dalai Lama.

22 Solidarity with Poland

Ever since 1951, when Polish children had been among the first refugees to come to "Ockenden," Joyce had had many Polish friends. She loved Polish people. She worried about them as, in 1980, Poland plunged into economic crisis.

On Easter Day 1981, she met Malcolm Stewart, administrator of Ockenden's Hindhead Vietnamese reception centre, in the lane, as both were on their way to an Easter prayer meeting at "Keffolds." "A thought just came to me in the bath, Malcolm," she said. "We must do something about Poland!"

Later, sitting in the spring sunshine in "Keffolds" terraced garden, Joyce and Malcolm discussed the dangerous situation that was developing. Solidarity, uniting workers of all trades, had become an increasingly militant force for democracy. A general strike had only just been averted by last-minute concessions from the communist government. Now, with the economy on the point of collapse, Solidarity was on a collision course with the regime.

Joyce thought, if only Polish people could feel the West's support and sympathy and believe that, one day, they would achieve their aspirations, they might hold back from outright rebellion. Rebellion would lead to a Russian invasion and to another surge of Polish refugees. "We have to let them know we care," said Joyce. Respecting Joyce's intuition, Malcolm drew a poster with the slogan "You can stop a tank."

Three months later, Joyce was guided, by a Franciscan nun, down a side aisle to the front of Poland's holiest shrine, the Church of the Black Madonna, in Czestochowa. Strangely, the dense crowd of pilgrims parted to let her through. Stranger still, a priest beckoned her to the centre. Standing at the altar rail, gazing at the ikon of the Black Madonna, Joyce knew that the prayers for her work in Poland would be answered.

Jill Buxton and many of Ockenden's long-standing Polish friends had helped Joyce to weave strands of coincidence and possibility into a plan for a fact-finding tour of Polish hospitals, welfare centres and children's institutions. Marta Zielinska, from the Laski Foundation for Blind Children, would direct Joyce from Warsaw across country to Cracow and back by a different route. When Joyce arrived in Poland, Marta was waiting at Warsaw airport to collect her and drive her to Laski.

Warsaw, destroyed by the Germans after the Polish uprising of 1944, had been rebuilt, stone by stone, statue by statue. Marta pointed out the palace of the Primate of Poland, where seventy-nine-year-old Cardinal Wysinski had recently died and the square where a quarter of a million mourners had gathered for his requiem mass. When the Catholic church was under persecution, the charismatic cardinal had been under house arrest for three years in a monastery. Now, after Cardinal Wysinski's death, Pope John Paul II, the first Polish pope, had called for thirty days' calm and mourning, announcing Archbishop Jozef Glemp as the cardinal's successor.

Nearly forty years after the war, Warsaw had come to life again. Pavement cafes were playing lively music and people were sitting outside, eating ice cream. All the same, lines of weary people led to empty-looking shops and long strings of cars queued at garages. Poland, a potentially rich, food-growing, northern country, was on the brink of a State of Emergency, the first developed country to be affected by what would become a global economic recession, the result of world-wide inflationary policies.

Polish home produce was being exported to meet the national debt, leaving supermarkets bare, except for vegetables. Meat, dairy products and baby foods, cooking oil, vitamin products, sugar and pulses were in short supply; washing products, nappies, cotton wool and toilet rolls were unobtainable.

In the green woods of Laski, gilded with bird song, sixty civilians and 200 Franciscan nuns in brown and black habits and novices in grey, were lovingly caring for 300 blind children. The Laski Community had survived Poland's invasion by Nazis and Russians. It would also outlast the atheistic communist regime. It had a farm (with chickens, pigs, bees and dogs), school buildings rebuilt after a forty-hour battle in 1944, and a square, cloistered hospital. Nuns' quarters were replacing camp-like huts.

Sister Maria Czacka, blind from the age of twenty-two, had founded the Laski Community, with the help of a Father Kornilowicz and of Marylska, a layman, who had come for a fortnight but stayed until he died, taking holy orders at the age of seventy. Now Miss Zofia Morawska, an elderly aristocratic lady, ran the community. She gave Joyce lunch in her wooden house which had red geraniums outside and vases of white daisies within. Sister Rozalia, who did the cooking, reminded Joyce of Mrs Rockaszynska at "Keffolds," in her enjoyment of their appreciation of her imaginative, attractively presented dishes.

Peering between the fronds of a giant, cascading fern onto a walled garden bright with roses, sweet-william and delphiniums, Joyce and Miss Morawska talked about Joyce's plans to help Poland. They discussed which Church and State-run institutions she should visit, which Government officials she should meet, and the possibility of Cardinal Glemp's confirming Poland's need for assistance if she were to contact England's Primate, Cardinal Hume.

After a peaceful night on the ground floor of a woodland building surrounded by geraniums, Joyce ate an early breakfast of cheese, honey, freshly baked brown bread and coffee with Miss Morawska. Then she embarked on her tour.

Courageous, dedicated people were working under extreme difficulty in all the institutions Joyce visited. In the main Warsaw hospital, Dr Kulaski, the doctor who had set up the Solidarity drugs bank, was looking after premature babies in the intensive care unit. There were no spare parts to repair two of six incubators which had broken down, allowing the children who had been inside them to die, Everywhere the problem was finance. The nuns at a convent home at Prvazkow had only twenty-five or thirty zlotys a day for each of ninety-one mentally handicapped boys.

At the Warsaw H.Q. of Solidarity, a former teachers' training college, Joyce learned of Poland's urgent need for baby food, powdered milk, semolina and drugs. The Solidarity Social Welfare Fund, which had only recently been established, was just beginning to find out about special needs and knew only of a few, expensive means of road transport. Joyce talked over the situation with Father Gialuk, who was in charge of supplies already coming from overseas and being stored and sorted out for distribution at the Church of the Sisters of Nazareth.

From Warsaw, Joyce travelled south, in a Caritas minibus, through unfinished, unpainted villages, to Kracow, in the company of a blind girl, two blind ladies, two kitchen helpers and two nuns. At least, the Polish harvest was good, in narrow strips of land, planted alternately with grain, onions, poppies and cabbages, and in allotments which people were tending with wooden hand hoes. In grassy ditches beside the road cows and horses were tethered, flocks of wild geese honked overhead and storks nested in the trees.

The flat, open fields further north gave way to forests, woods and hills near Kracow whose black crumbling buildings were overhung with grey smoke from the Novabuta steel works. Joyce, staying in a convent in a room recently used by Pope John Paul II, was embarrassed at being waited on by elderly, dignified sisters. Once again she was reminded of Mrs Rockaszynska by the joy one of the nuns took in preparing appetising food.

Near Kracow, two under–staffed, under–supplied state homes for social rejects and for the elderly and handicapped were run by nuns and brothers of an order founded by Brother Bernard Chmielowski, an artist who dedicated his life to the poor. Joyce found that they needed vitamins and clothes.

In 1973, Cardinal Wojtyla, now the Pope, had started a home just outside Krakow for unmarried, expectant mothers, to discourage them from having State-facilitated abortions. The Sisters of Nazareth had at first given up their own rooms for the girls, then the Church had purchased a villa for the expectant mothers and another for new mothers and babies on their return from hospital. The girls could hand their babies over to an adoption society, but in the end few did so. Though no pressure was put on them to become believers, following the nuns' example, they often attended mass in each house's chapel. Joyce noted the homes' shortage of clothing, layettes, nappies and baby food.

It was at this stage in her journey that Joyce went to pray in the chapel of the Black Madonna whose face was familiar from a reproduction of the ikon on the wall at "Keffolds." The memory of the Madonna's sanctity sustained her afterwards, as she visited the former concentration camp of Oeschien-Auschwitz in the company of tourists who had brought flowers. She walked through the infamous gate, under the inscription, "Arbeit macht frei" (work makes you free) and past the crematorium. Not far away, a happier memorial, the Pope's birthplace, had been spruced up and turned into a tourist centre.

Back at Laski, tormented by the conflicting emotions aroused by her various visits, Joyce was unable to sleep. She lay listening to dogs barking and to thunder resounding in the woods.

First thing in the morning, she joined nuns and villagers for mass in a fir–log chapel where vases of daisies stood on a green altar cloth. Then she was driven 120 kilometres to a pleasant, though institutional, home for sixty children, in a country mansion at Sitdlee. There were no toys, except for an identical yellow dog on every bed.

Joyce and the nuns said fond goodbyes — Joyce making them a donation, Miss Morawska writing a message for Czeslaw, a Polish member of Ockenden's community and Sister Rozalia sending him Polish roses.

On her return to England, a letter Joyce wrote to *The Observer* about Poland, though not an appeal, resulted in £16,000 being sent to The Ockenden Venture, in small cheques. It was the answer she had been looking for, proving that an extraordinary determination and energy to help Poland was gathering momentum. Joyce approached Doris Brown, head of Ockenden's finance office, to open a Polish fund.

The Red Cross, Christian Aid and Oxfam gave Ockenden helpful advice on running an aid campaign involving bulk overseas shipment. Ockenden had innumerable facilities and a mass of expertise of its own to call upon — an army of people whom Joyce had collected to help the Vietnamese. They were on stand-by, needing only to be asked, to launch themselves into a Polish campaign.

There was also a Mr Mirzinski. For two years, even during the time of Poland's military government, he made a fleet of Polish Government trucks available in ones and twos to Ockenden and other Polish Aid projects, delivering direct to the Church and other non-governmental distribution networks in Poland.

The first Ockenden pantechnicon and its precious contents were to be sent for distribution to a place of unimpeachable integrity — the Laski Blind School. Helpers in Woking, watching the truck loaded up, were shocked at the paltry heap the goods they had collected made in its cavernous interior. Joyce standing there, hands on hips, asked in disbelief, "Is this all?" As the implications of going into aid shipment suddenly became plain, she sent Czes and Joe, another Pole, to the nearest supermarket with an open cheque to buy it out of baby food and dry goods. An astonished manager sold products to the value of £2,000.

Miss Morawska sent her thanks and deep gratitude to Joyce, not only for what she was doing but also for her "unquenchable spirit which puts optimism into our hearts."

Nationally and internationally, people threw themselves into collecting goods for Poland, stuffing them into garages and cramming them into huts, houses and hallways. Charles Wheeler, the BBC correspondent, rang Ockenden for help. He had appealed for shoes and was marooned in the bandstand at Godalming with 10,000 pairs. "I could have told him," Joyce said, "Never appeal for shoes! I did that once. Never again!"

Though she was deeply involved in events, as always Joyce avoided taking up any political position. She was less interested in EEC aid (though it too relied on voluntary help, free lorries and free storage facilities) than in despatching what had been donated, collected, stored, organised and shipped by groups of individuals. Yet Ockenden had an important part to play in the EEC aid programme.

Amid increasing unrest, Polish factories ran out of raw materials: currency became worthless: food queues began sleeping in the streets. On 13th December, General Jaruzelski imposed martial law, crushing Solidarity and imprisoning 10,000 people, including Solidarity's leader, Lech Walesa. Tanks stormed the Lenin shipyard. In Wujek colliery, seven miners were killed.

As the Polish border was sealed, an Ockenden lorry was only a few miles away. Would it get through? A convoy of 100 trucks arrived, whose Dutch drivers, having obtained a promise from a Dutch supermarket chain to match anything they could raise, had brought two million gilders' worth of supplies. The sheer volume of their presence reopened the border, through which, tucked in somewhere at the back of the column, slipped the Ockenden truck.

Western governments, outraged by General Jaruzelski's action, imposed economic and political sanctions, exacerbating Poland's economic problems. The EEC Charity Commission withheld £16,000,000 it had allocated for Poland, in case it fell into the hands of the military.

Only ordinary citizens of the world, through voluntary agencies, provided a life–line of support. Joyce begged people to allow compassion to rise above politics; to become channels for answers to Polish prayers.

The EEC decided to distribute the £16,000,000 aid in the form of supplies sent directly to institutions by the non–governmental organisations. Representing Ockenden at the meeting for EEC NGOs, Malcolm sat silent, rather out of his depth, behind a desk plaque saying "United Kingdom," listening to interpreters translating the wheelings and dealings of old agency hands for a share of the relief budget.

At the end of the meeting, the chairman approached Malcolm, saying, "I was wondering which agency you represent?" Hearing that it was Ockenden, he said, "Oh, Joyce! We shall, of course, be distributing funds to you." Together with the Sue Ryder Foundation, Ockenden was given £114,000 a month, with which to buy meat, oil, sugar, pulses, toiletries and baby milk.

Ockenden's army again came into action after a television programme on Poland. Joyce took part in a meeting between programme makers and agencies involved, apparently dozing most of the time but, in reality, registering everything of importance. She arranged for 2,000 Ockenden and Rotary centres up and down the country to store the goods which poured in, for the transportation of which Mr Mirzinski supplied trucks. As Ockenden trucks reached double figures, The Venture became, until 1984, the co–ordinating agency for all English efforts on behalf of Poland and for fostering voluntary initiatives inside Poland.

To comply with EEC Charity Commission regulations, in May 1982, Caroline Shaw, who worked with Malcolm Stewart, travelled to Poland with two Ockenden trucks, each carrying twenty tons of EEC food and toiletries. Loaded in Farnham, they were driven by English drivers to Harwich, then put on a ferry to be collected by German drivers at Hamburg. Caroline travelled out on the truck destined for Czestochowa and returned on the other as it returned from Sandomierz.

Though Caroline felt depressed during the first part of the long, spartan journey, once she reached Czestochowa her spirits brightened. Her impression of Poland was transformed. The peace and beauty radiating from the face of the Black Madonna she found also in the eyes of Bishop Domin, to whom goods were directed. He compared the history of Poland with the mysteries of the rosary. The joyful mysteries were in tune with the recent happiness and optimism in Poland. The sorrowful mysteries resembled the current suppression and sadness of Polish people. The glorious mysteries were like the time of freedom in Poland which was still to come.

When, later in the year, Joyce and Jill Buxton crossed the border from East Germany, the soldiers on the Polish side searched the Land Rover for guns and munitions, opened all packages, examined the vehicle's under-carriage and, after trying to decipher it for three and a half hours, confiscated Caroline's report.

In Wroclaw, watching television in the flat of some friends, Joyce and Jill were startled by low-flying helicopters. They ran outside, Joyce reminded of a wartime novel, *It Could Happen Here*, as "special police" jumped down from four army trucks, closed the road and took charge of banks and post offices. While the helicopters continued to roar overhead, soldiers began checking all young men, asking why they were there, demanding to see their passes, maintaining control by terror and humiliation. Back in the flat the family remained unconcerned, accepting the events of the last half hour as a matter of course.

Praying in the chapel at Czestochowa a second time, on the anniversary of the miracle of the Black Madonna, Joyce could feel the longing of the people for a free Poland, as they prayed, wept and walked on their knees behind the altar. Yet, at Laski, the nuns were as serene as ever. On the day martial law began, they had come to the rescue of some young boy soldiers, in shoddy uniforms, who had lost their way in the forest. They had given them food and helped them.

In Bishop Domin's absence, Jill and Joyce learned that he needed ground sheets, games, pencils and writing books for children's summer camps he was organising. Yet he thought baby food an even greater priority. Undernourished mothers could not feed their babies and the infant mortality rate was rising.

After the Pope's second visit to Poland in 1983, martial law ended. An amnesty for political prisoners opened the way for political contact with the West. Basic foods began to reach Polish shops, though at prices few could afford. Rickets returned because of a lack of vitamins and TB cases multiplied. Dedicated care in the overcrowded hospitals prevented patients from developing bed sores, but there were few antibiotics to counter post-operative infection. Hepatitis increased because of the re-using of needles and syringes.

In Woking, packing, preparing and organising continued, spreading into Ruth Hicks's house, with Ruth and fiery Czeslaw Chmielinski, who lived there, at the heart of it. Czes, brought to England as a young man by Sue Ryder, had been in revolt against the world, including his well-wishers and rescuers, and full of anger about his years in a German labour camp. Yet he was devoted to the Ockenden community into which he had come in 1955. Ockenden's Polish children loved and respected him and Ruth Hicks treasured him as a son.

Czes sat the Polish lorry drivers down to huge bacon and egg breakfasts, then marshalled muscle among Ockenden's young Poles and central Europeans, doing a lion's share of carrying himself. He also raised enough money — by a pigeon auction — to become a founding beneficiary of a Warsaw children's home.

The Poland Fund reconnected Czes with his roots, healing his memories. For the first time for forty years, he returned to Poland with Malcolm Stewart, who was visiting Katovice, the nerve centre of the Church's relief distribution. While Malcolm, as Joyce's representative, was placed in the front row of two million people, for a mass conducted through thunder and rain from a seventy-foot pyramid by the Pope, Czes had a dramatic experience of his own.

Visiting his home village, he asked someone to identify the house where his sister had lived, before she died at Auschwitz. Not only did the man know the house, he also knew Czes's sister who was alive and well and down the road doing her shopping. By the time Czes met Malcolm again, his life had completely changed.

Having already suffered two heart attacks, Czes suffered a final, fatal one on Easter Day 1986, a year after Joyce's death and six weeks after Ruth Hicks died. He bequeathed the money he had made from racing pigeons and a legacy from Ruth to The Ockenden Venture. It was enough to equip a new ward, complete with twenty incubators, in the impoverished children's hospital in Lublin.

It was not only the aid distributed to Poland but, more importantly, the friendship and concern of ordinary people which it demonstrated that first built bridges between East and West Europe. It proved the truth of Joyce's vision. Beneath political confrontation, communication of the spirit can spring from person to person, opening floodgates of human understanding.

23 A Strategy of Hope for a World in Crisis

The Ockenden Venture and all other agencies, large and small, governmental and non-governmental, solved only a fraction of the problems that arose in the second half of the twentieth century. Every year, it seemed, there was more intolerance and cruelty in the world and more people became refugees.

Even so, despite all the evil and suffering and despite the spread of nuclear weapons, Joyce became convinced that God was guiding mankind towards a state of universal harmony. His creative dynamic, not detectable in terms of individual human lives or even in the lives of nations, was working through millions of souls to bring the group soul to perfection. The vast movement of peoples in modern times was part of this process. Refugees, forced to settle in new countries, had no choice but to work towards multi-racial understanding.

Most importantly to Joyce as a Western Christian, the message of brotherly love was at last getting through to young people. In the past, Christianity had been so "other-worldly" that it had been called the "opiate of the people". At worst it had been used as an excuse for persecution. All that had changed. Young volunteers now coming to Ockenden believed in human rights and equality of opportunity. In the twentieth century global village, they found it natural to extend this love to their brothers and sisters in the Third World, the developing countries as they are now known.

At the same time, young people understood that the universe was a system of ever-moving components, in which, acting and inter-acting according to free will, they modified their own and other people's lives. What they did affected the fragile planet itself, on which all living things depend. In a new, ecological age, beneath the movements of politics, the Holy Spirit was clearly and simply guiding people towards healing lives and towards conserving the earth.

The concept of wholeness had been transmitted over many centuries. Five hundred years before Christ, Buddha had taught detachment from selfish needs in order to cultivate responsibility and concern for the whole. Six hundred and fifty years later, 150 years after Christ, the Emperor Marcus Aurelius had seen the world as "an animated being" and had spoken of a "universal sense running through the whole mass of matter."

What seemed particularly significant to Joyce was that the concept of wholeness was for the first time being understood in the West — where communications and technology had first advanced, where Christ had chosen to be "earthed" and where he had predicted that man would perform miracles of healing like his own ("...the works that I do shall ye do also; and greater works than these shall ye do"). Of course, it was still horribly possible that instead of grasping positive opportunities, man would use his free will negatively, to blast or pollute himself and the earth into poisonous dust.

The way for the human race to avoid this ultimate catastrophe was to recreate, on a grand scale, the "net-working" of ordinary people of good will. By this means, "Having stepped," Joyce said, "onto an energy field of love", Ockenden had been empowered to help so many seemingly hopeless situations. Just as after the war Joyce had introduced a new dimension into sixth form education, so now, in 1984, she launched an educational initiative to increase global consciousness — "A Strategy of Hope for a World in Crisis", the culmination of her thinking over the years.

At a meeting in the House of Commons, addressed by Prince Sadruddin Aga Khan, she asked people from the fields of humanitarian issues, education, healing, employment, youth, ecology, the media and the arts, to lobby for a change; for Britain, with its tradition of freedom of speech and voluntary service, to lead the world in revolutionising teaching in schools. It was vital, she felt, to capitalize on what students already knew by giving them a new, non-insular perspective, making them intellectually aware of continuing global problems and of the urgent need to solve them.

When young people had a clear, rational overview of the world, they would be far more effective in solving its problems than their parents had been. Ockenden could have done nothing without the massive support of the well-meaning older generation of the British public. That support had, all the same, been spasmodic; on an emotional, rather than an intellectual level; flooding in only when, and because, television high-lighted some particular group of suffering people.

Once the younger generation really understood that suffering was going on all the time somewhere, a far wider "net-working" would, she believed, reach out to every corner of the earth where human rights were being violated. It would be an outlet for the creative energy of the young on which Ockenden had always depended, which, in other circumstances, could spend itself in protest marches or wars. Giving a few years to solving global problems would provide young people with an alternative to slotting straight into the capitalist system, perhaps preventing many who were disillusioned or unemployed from resorting to violence or drug-taking or from excessively following fashion.

Sadly, little more than a year after setting this strategy to "transmute the earth to a higher vibration of love, concern and compassion" in motion, Joyce died of cancer. Death, as nothing in life could ever do, forced her to delegate the projection of her vision of how ordinary people could help refugees, wherever they lived in the world.

Joyce's international Ockenden family was stunned at the loss of her boundless energy and determination, her laughter, quicksilver inspirations, wry comments and capacity for always being late — but always in time. Gradually, painfully, it came to terms with its loss. In its flexible, non-institutional way, it continued developing Joyce's projects and starting new ones.

Lines which Joyce herself often quoted convey her message of warning, hope and resolution, as well as her profound trust in the goodwill of the young. They were written by a seventeen–year–old Cypriot girl, whose way of life had been destroyed by political, religious and racial tension.

> The world is like a crystal ball, ready
> To smash into pieces at any moment.
> We, the young generation,
> Hold the ball in our hands.
> We mustn't let it crash.
> We can fight for this,
> We can keep the ball still.
> Well, let's fight!
> We are holding the world in our hands.
> We can stop war and hate and bring
> Back the missing love.
> Yes we can, because
> Life and the World belong to us.

"What a sound idea," Joyce would have said, "for a young person to have the last word!" It had been, after all, a group of seventeen– and eighteen–year–olds who had changed her life and the lives of thousands of others by asking her, all those years ago, "Couldn't we give a few refugees a holiday?"